GOING WHERE
I'M COMING
FROM

## OTHER PERSEA ANTHOLOGIES

AMERICA STREET: A MULTICULTURAL ANTHOLOGY OF STORIES
*Edited by Anne Mazer*

FIRST SIGHTINGS: CONTEMPORARY STORIES OF AMERICAN YOUTH
*Edited by John Loughery*

INTO THE WIDENING WORLD: INTERNATIONAL COMING-OF-AGE STORIES
*Edited by John Loughery*

IMAGINING AMERICA: STORIES FROM THE PROMISED LAND
*Edited by Wesley Brown and Amy Ling*

VISIONS OF AMERICA: PERSONAL NARRATIVES FROM THE PROMISED LAND
*Edited by Wesley Brown and Amy Ling*

PAPER DANCE: 55 LATINO POETS
*Edited by Victor Hernández Cruz, Leroy V. Quintana, and Virgil Suarez*

POETS FOR LIFE: SEVENTY-SIX POETS RESPOND TO AIDS
*Edited by Michael Klein*

IN THE COMPANY OF MY SOLITUDE:
AMERICAN WRITING FROM THE AIDS PANDEMIC
*Edited by Marie Howe and Michael Klein*

Memoirs of American Youth

Edited by Anne Mazer

A Karen and Michael Braziller Book
PERSEA BOOKS/NEW YORK

*With gratitude, the publisher and the editor wish to acknowledge Wesley Brown, who contributed the title to this volume.*



*For information, contact the publisher:*
*Persea Books, Inc.*
*853 Broadway*
*New York, New York 10003*

*Library of Congress Cataloging-in-Publication Data*
*Going where I'm coming from: memoirs of American youth / edited by Anne Mazer.*
*p. cm.*
*ISBN 0-89255-205-0 : $15.95*
*ISBN 0-89255-206-9 (pbk.): $6.95*
*1. Authors, American—20th century—Biography—Juvenile literature. 2. Youth—United States—Biography—Juvenile literature. [1. Authors, American. 2. Identity.] I. Mazer, Anne.*
*PS129.G65 1994*
*818′.540308—dc20*
*[B] 94-15595*
*CIP*
*AC*

*Designed by REM Studio, Inc.*
*Typeset in Zapf International Light by ComCom, Allentown, Pennsylvania*
*Printed on acid-free, recycled paper and bound by The Haddon Craftsmen, Bloomsburg, Pennsylvania*
*Jacket and cover printed by Lynn Art, New York, New York*

**7 8 9 10 RRD 06 05**

# CONTENTS

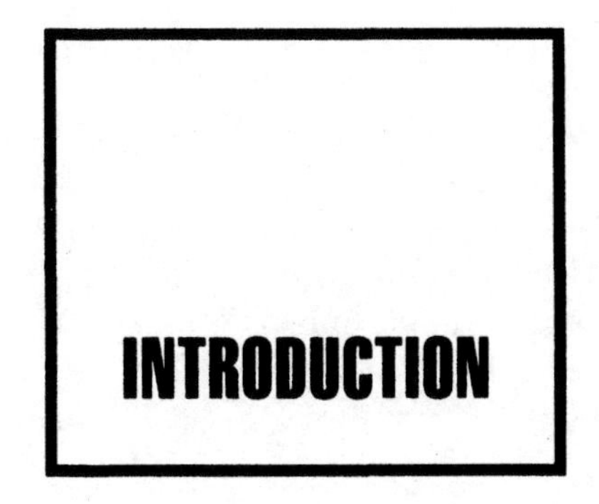

# INTRODUCTION

We all love stories of childhood and youth—especially when they are true. They not only offer a unique look at the personal and historical forces which shape us, but they also illuminate the complex and ever-changing interaction between self and society. As the narratives of *Going Where I'm Coming From* will attest, that interaction is even more subtle and complex in the United States, where personal identity is forged in the crucible of a multiethnic society.

Through memoirs and essays, many of them published here for the first time, the writers of *Going Where I'm Coming From* explore a wide range of experiences. Some tell what it's like to immigrate to the United States as a young person. Others address the difficulties and richness of growing up within two cultures. Still others reflect on cultural aspects of family ties, school experiences, prejudice, and male and female stereotypes.

In "Always Running," Luis J. Rodríguez gives a very contemporary account of immigration. He tells of crossing the border from Mexico with his family as a young child to live in the Los Angeles barrio (Watts), and how he and his brothers absorbed the code of the streets in order to survive. In "Sound-Shadows of the New World," fifteen-year-old Ved Mehta comes to America alone. Blind since early infancy, he leaves his close-knit, traditional family in India and travels to New York City on his way to the Arkansas School for the Blind. His adjustment is rendered in a humorous and bittersweet tone. Judith Ortiz Cofer lives in double exile, both from her native Puerto Rico and from the Puerto Rican barrio in New Jersey. In "One More Lesson," Cofer comes to understand the power of language when she is punished in school for not understanding instructions given only in English.

The experiences of first-generation Americans are explored from different vantage points. In "Dinnertime," Helen Epstein, growing up in New York City with her Czech Jewish parents who have both survived the Nazi concentration camps of the Second World War, describes the tensions of a home life overshadowed by a tragic past. Tracy Marx takes a humorous, affectionate look at living with her Polish mother in "Absolutely Someday," and comes to appreciate her mother's wisdom. Hisaye Yamamoto's "The Enormous Piano" shimmers with memories as she looks back over her childhood in a Japanese-American family that moves from farm to farm in California. In "One Last Time," Gary Soto describes long summers spent in the fields of Northern California as a migrant worker with his mother, brother, and sister.

Many of the writers address cultural issues beyond immigration. Lensey Namioka, Graham Salisbury, and Willie Ruff all question entrenched societal attitudes. In her essay "Math and After Math," Namioka writes about being female and excelling at math—something expected in China, but not in the United States. Graham Salisbury examines images of manhood on a

Hawaiian island through his relationship with a succession of stepfathers in "Ice." Jazz musician Willie Ruff's early fascination with sound, in "A Call to Assembly," leads him to explore sign language and the world of the deaf in rural Alabama, and ultimately to reject limiting concepts of himself based on race.

A fascination with family history unites Lee A. Daniels and Susan Power. Daniels, in "A Boston Latin School Boy," tells of his growing awareness of the civil rights movement and of his identity as a black person, while simultaneously being nurtured by the classical education he received at Boston Latin School, a traditional, mostly white school. In "Stone Women," Susan Power, a member of the Standing Rock Sioux tribe, seamlessly interweaves the history of her Native American forebears with her own life. She focuses particularly on her mother and aunt, and on others such as her great-great grandfather Two Bears, a chief who led the Battle of White Stone Hill in 1863.

*Going Where I'm Coming From* begins and ends with key pieces. In "Wings," Thylias Moss writes about accompanying her mother to her work as a maid, struggling against the low expectations her school held for a young black girl, and witnessing death—an odyssey that leads her first into silence and finally to the transcending power of her own voice. A fitting conclusion to the collection is offered by "Thank You in Arabic," Naomi Shihab Nye's story of the year her parents left St. Louis and took the family to live in Jerusalem with her Arab relatives. There she adapts to an ancient way of life—though she is often homesick and rebels against the strict limitations on women and girls. When Nye returns to the United States, however, she discovers a new kind of homesickness, and realizes that her stay has forever transformed her definitions of home, country, and self.

Like Naomi Shihab Nye, the other writers of *Going Where I'm Coming From* all take a journey to find out who they are. For some, it is a journey influenced by events of history. Others examine the choices they made while young that set a course for their lives. Many describe painful experiences that nevertheless have given them strength and wisdom. To find out who they are and where they're going, the writers of this collection have

# WINGS

## Thylias Moss

THYLIAS MOSS teaches at the University of Michigan in Ann Arbor where she lives with her husband and two young sons. The recipient of many literary prizes, she has published six books, including the poetry collections *Rainbow Remnants in Rock Bottom Ghetto Sky* and *Small Congregations*, and *I Want to Be*, a picture book for children.

My mother seemed to love getting out of the house, maybe because she couldn't think of herself without thinking also of travel, being named, as she is, after two states. Florida and Missouri, sunshine and show me. Most of the time, she tended to flowers in the yard and raised onions and tomatoes in sections of the lawn difficult for my father to mow because of the slope. But she was outside, even if she just sat on the porch or on a blanket under the fruit trees we had; all but one bore deep purple plums the shape of tears and of the most delicate Christmas ornaments we had, that we looked at in their cushioned nests but never handled and never dared hang on the tree, so that I'd have them for my children and they for their children. I do have children now, but those ornaments somehow got away from me.

It would have been better to suspend them from pine branches, maybe putting pillows under the tree in case they fell; it would have been better to let the ornaments be the decorations they were meant to be, catching the sunlight and throwing it around the room in rainbows. But we didn't. Loss is not always terrible; sometimes the longing that loss creates is within me—a low hum, a tiny motor turning, operating, supplying me with power.

In Tennessee, my mother had worked in a dry cleaners and in the hat factory where many of her eleven brothers and sisters eventually worked for a while. There are no photographs of her childhood, her adolescence; no pictures of the happy couple the night that she and my father became engaged, not one wedding picture. For those moments, I have only my powers of investigation. I become a detective, conducting deep searches into her face when she falls asleep, more and more easily now, while we talk or attempt to watch a film together. I take away lines, yellowing of the eyes, pounds; I blacken her hair, lengthen it, braid it in my thoughts and tie ribbons on it, ribbons made from the reeds that grew by the creek she walked by as she walked the miles to the colored school until she stopped going, having learned, she was told, all a colored girl would ever need to know.

She was good at basketball and at art; I have drawings of hers from ninth-grade biology, her last year of school, illustrations of frogs and paramecia that look like diagrams from impressive reference books, so detailed are they. But I've been to that house she grew up in. There was a living room, a bedroom, a kitchen, a mother, a father until he was killed (the polite word), and twelve children. There was no way for her to draw during the day, no space, no time either for the fifth-born who had to be involved in household matters; laundry to be done in the same steel tubs they bathed in, water to be heated on the wood and, much later, gas stove. I imagine that it was only at night, maybe after she woke from her pallet on the floor to go to the outhouse, that she didn't want to go back to sleep but wanted instead to draw at the table in the kitchen that every other hour of the day had to be put to practical purpose. Pencils and paper that she hid under her pallet were pulled out and the bare bulb in the kitchen turned on. My next gifts to her will be canvas, easel, and oil paint; a note that says, "Find it again."

How different it was at my father's house in many, many ways. His was a family of mixed bloods, the mother brown as honey, the father brown only if he worked in the sun; not a colored man. They lived not far from my mother's house, literally midway between the white section and the colored section called the Bottom. My Aunt Cora, my mother's youngest sister, inherited the family's small house in the Bottom. Every summer, until I was thirteen, I would visit both of my grandmothers, my aunts, and cousins. My cousin Tony and I would walk to the gas station—the town had only one—to use the bathroom. Eventually we were given our own key. For bathing, Tony didn't want her modern cousin with long hair and long (about an inch and real) fingernails from up North to use a steel tub in the front yard as she did, so we walked up the hill to Miss Helen's house that smelled like a spice forest. Her soap smelled good too. Back at Tony's house, her sisters and brothers, who were too proud to bathe in Miss Helen's swan-footed tub, would sit near us to sniff in secret our skin.

Up that same hill I walked to Grandma Leila's white house and the porch that wrapped around three sides of it. My father's was a family of property. I remember important-looking (dress shirts and dark ties) white men driving up in late-model cars and knocking on her door. I don't know what they wanted. I remember books in that house and space, pictures on the walls, braided rugs, three bedrooms, a living room, dining room, a kitchen almost as large as the whole house my mother's family inhabited. I remember in the yard geese white and fat as the pillows on the beds. I remember a photograph of me standing on the steps of that house, a photograph of the pale grandfather I never knew, my father a baby in his arms. I remember a photograph of my father young, a brimmed hat cocked to the side—he looked like a sailor, like someone easy for my mother to fall in love with. My father enjoyed indoor plumbing all his life, but an outhouse was still standing, a kind of memorial.

Grandma Leila Taylor Brasier was a descendent of abolitionists of Philadelphia; it was work in Civil Rights that brought her parents to Tennessee. It was work in Civil Rights she did until she couldn't work anymore. When I was five, Grandma Leila ordered the outhouse torn down. She wanted to fight forward without spending so much time looking back to the past; she could see that much further ahead if she wasn't turning around all the time, going backwards. My father, a high school graduate, tore it down with his bare hands. I sat on the ground shelling peanuts. The sunflowers around me were like bright cameras of dozens of reporters eager not to miss a little minor history.

When my parents migrated north as so many blacks did in the fifties, my mother became a maid, and I went to work with her sometimes. I folded my hands at the kitchen tables where she wouldn't let me eat though I wanted to badly; our kitchen table did not have the elegant scrolled legs or the cherry and oak tops whose wood grains were so fine they were like an artist's signature. I wanted to know if the peanut butter or egg salad would taste different on such tables; I knew I would bite the sandwiches differently, that I'd try for the most distinguished chewing possible, chewing without moving my mouth or jaw. Our dining room table was as dark a wood as cherry because my mother stained it that way, and the day she did, her palm was as brown as the outside of her hand. She would buy white plaster birds and paint them brighter than what birds we had: pigeons, sparrows, wrens, the occasional cardinal and blue jay, and first thing in the morning, ravens and crows. The flowers were as bright as the best birds. There are too many rainbows in her house; they tangle, don't distinguish themselves the way she wants them to.

We ate instead in the cool emergency stairway of the high-rise on Cleveland's Gold Coast, spreading Cannon towels over our laps. We'd order elaborate dishes from the menus we'd packed and would tell unusually tall waiters (we'd tilt our heads all the way back) to hurry as we had to return to the office in just half an hour; our work was much too important for us to be away any longer, and there was no one else who could do it as well. These were menus we'd made during my embroidery lessons though she didn't call them lessons. In those cool stairways, wrapped up in so much dim grayness, we found the place inside ourselves that we could always come back to. There would be times when a woman named Florida Missouri would want to go somewhere simple, where words we spoke would be like stones skipped on the water to fall with mild echoes to the bottom.

I saw only the women my mother worked for, the wives, but for some reason I never thought it odd. To this day, I can't picture them with husbands or even with fathers. It seems natural only when I picture them alone, or if not alone, then with my mother who sometimes would do their hair and comment on its fineness: it was impossible to hold a single strand; when she thought she had one, it was at least a dozen, some of them twisted around her finger. She would say a ring was not practical; she'd have to remove it so as not to pull out their hair that really was white, like beige and ivory, like their often age-spotted skin. She said she was glad she didn't have a ring, that a ring was not the best way to know that she was married. But the night I became engaged, she held the ring, turning it over and over in the light for an hour. She kept asking if it were real; she meant the world, its wonders, a small piece of which she was holding even though she'd have to give it up to me, the person it was meant for.

My mother was never able to come home from work without bags of things these women would give her: lots of clothes, shoes, handbags, jewelry, knickknacks, kitchen gadgets and ceramic ware, and food. She'd be given furniture too, paintings, books, too, but these things did not come every day. When she had enough of them locked away, she'd get someone with a van or light truck to help her take them home. We didn't have a car. My father claimed to have had a Mercury, a Studebaker, but only before I was born. After that, he didn't need to hold a steering wheel; it seems that until the day he died there was no place else he wanted to go. And on that day, I rushed him to the hospital in a car—I meant to rush, it felt like rushing, though it did no good, a car, first car I ever had. I rode to work with my mother on the bus and dreamed dreams for the people I saw, most of their faces so sour-looking I didn't think it was possible that they dreamed dreams for themselves.

It is as if my mother lives in a museum, the Kitsch Hall of Fame on Durkee Avenue. She accepts graciously all these women give her, no matter that these gifts be junk, worth but a few faltering dollars. Giving is all that some of these women can do; the only talent of these widows. My mother would admire the fine quality of what she was given as if such goods were seldom her own, and could not ever be without their generosity. Even if it were a coat or dress too many years out of style—and unattractive even had it been in style. Even if, though beautiful, it were unflattering to her rich coloring that is like rum relieved with lots of ochre, lots of yellow. I just like the warm sound of *rum;* it is what her color felt like when she hugged me. There are other words that describe the color better, but not the feeling, and the feeling is much more important. By now, her house is furnished entirely with gifts. In the dining room is a fifty-gallon glass tank that once was the home of tropical fish, but now it is home to gaudy plastic flowers, plastic fruit, wooden eggs, cut-glass pieces of chandelier, bills, a hand-carved bust of a beatnik, and Christmas cards. Dresses, some of them evening gowns she hopes to find a reason to wear, bring to her closet the perfumes of other women, sweetness and stories that won't wash out. The rest she gives away.

Some of the women are so old now, they are giving away things they aren't through with, things more difficult to part with, things of greater personal value, but they are feeling the pressure of time and they want to see to it that my mother, who has visited some of them more than their own families have, gets special recognition. The service she provides has not been just maid service after all; it has been friendship. They still send clothes for me. I still say thank you, then give most of it to charity, to flood and hurricane relief efforts. Like my mother, I try not to mind that they see first my color and, because of it, assume that I must need assistance. There is a bronze, a goldenness that supports my brown; it looks as if sunset or the best of autumn is trying to push through my skin. It is color that should be seen. Glorious color.

Most of the time, traveling for my mother just meant getting out of her house and going to another, either to work or to God's house where she also worked: cooking, cleaning, ushering, singing, bookkeeping, praying. She was at church for the Wednesday prayer service, for the Thursday and Friday choir rehearsals, for Baptist Training Union meeting, and all day on Sunday for Sunday school, morning worship, afternoon program, and evening service. I went with her from the beginning of my life. While we were gone, my father completed the last hours of the ten hours necessary for the perfect cooking of pinto beans, onions cut up in them like small teeth. We came home to those beans, a cast-iron skillet of corn bread, his secret recipe slaw.

True Vine Baptist Church changed my life in unexpected ways. I was only five in my first clear memories of going there, so it was suspect just how much religion someone who couldn't tie her shoes (I was left-handed and had trouble with the right-handed lessons) could get. It was impossible, however, not to get something just by being in the presence of the choir robed in magenta satin and in the presence of all the hats, all the opulence of Sunday finery. For me what made Sundays exceptional was the man elevated in the center front of the sanctuary, golden white lights turned upon him, the rest of the sanctuary dim and cool. He wore white robes with gold brocade tippets, and the sleeves were full as wings; as he gestured through his sermons and speeches, he seemed to be flying. Then there was his voice itself, soothing as distant thunder, then loud and pointed as if his tongue were a whip, then rhythmic and hypnotic like singing and dance, a hula of the voice. It was delicious when those sounds entered my ears and filled them. With just his voice he was able to bring women and men in the congregation to tears. They would shout and writhe, jump and run through the aisles, or simply stand and quiver, so overwhelmed were they by the power and intensity of the spirit that the voice of the minister stirred within them. And I was mesmerized and awed; I learned what a voice could command; I learned just what a force of words could do, how words could touch and hammer and catapult and bring down joy like rain. I wanted to do that, too. Only with words. Nothing but words. I could get words easily; no one and nothing could keep words out of my mind, my mouth, my hands once I started to write them down. I could go anywhere with words, the places my mother is named for, the places she'll never see.

Although I stopped talking in school in fourth grade, I still wrote words, and so did not lose myself. We moved, in the middle of fourth grade, to a house on Durkee Avenue, homeowners for the first time, in a safer, mostly white, mostly Croatian neighborhood, and I almost immediately went from being an outgoing, popular girl to a withdrawn, shy, almost invisible girl. I don't know for sure why I stopped talking, why I would not speak up for myself and did not learn to do so again until I was in college, but it seems likely that it had to do with the way I was judged in the new school without my even opening up my mouth once. My mother had lost her art and I was losing mine, too.

In the new school, I was placed in a regular classroom although I'd been in accelerated classrooms since first grade. The violin I had been given in first grade was taken away. The French I had studied also since first grade was discontinued. New teachers and principals did not know that I had been selected for private instruction at the Phyllis Wheatley Institute beyond the once-a-week music lessons in my school. New teachers and principals did not know that I was thinking about becoming a concert violinist among many things I was thinking about becoming. They did not know, did not ask, and I did not tell, although I could have. Now a grown woman with children, I still want to be a concert violinist but can't get past how fulfillment of a dream was so easily fractured by assumptions that a little black girl was somehow not as capable as paler children being educated in a better, more affluent public school. They did not know; they did not ask; I did not tell them that in second grade I had given an oral report on Susan B. Anthony for which

I made protest signs and had girls march around the classroom dressed in old clothes from Janice Skipper's attic with only the flashlights they held for illumination. After I spoke, I marched with them, carrying a sign and chanting the poem I wrote. They didn't know, didn't ask, and I didn't tell them just how much thunder was in my voice as I spoke about equality for women. A seven-year-old girl in the inner city did this, a girl believing she could make anything happen until she moved to a better place and found out how utterly ordinary she was. Brown as a curled-up leaf off the tree, a nuisance on the lawn, raked into a heap for an autumn bonfire.

Yet I was happy. Though I had slit open the mouth of a life-size (three-foot-tall) doll so that she would be able to speak, though I had prayed the doll would come to life, and then, believing the prayer was about to be answered, grew terrified and broke off some of her fingers so that I could prove there was no bone, no blood, no life all the way up her hollow plastic arm, I was happy. A girl who had walked to the library when she was seven, loving books so much, and on the way there, had watched helplessly as a boy on a bicycle shiny as a promise (it must have been new) was struck down by a truck. I was the only witness, the one police talked to, the one who had a voice and used it, though the voice could do nothing for the boy except remember him.

I saw worse things, too, fire ravaging an apartment building, the flames spreading like a peacock's tail, so beautiful and then thick black smoke erasing the beauty, reminding me of the horror of the fire. For a long time, I could not use my parents' gas stove; I did not believe the fire would confine itself to the burners or would be satisfied just grilling a sandwich. I saw a girl jump out of a window to save herself from something in her apartment that was worse in her mind than crashing into the ground. I saw this and once again had only a voice. I saw what I did not want to see, accidents and deliberate acts of violence against people and property. I was happy nevertheless, going to work with my mother, ironing our menus, eating my father's slaw, listening to him sing like Bing Crosby and speak like President Kennedy, and walking with him to an underpass where I would say my name and it would be amplified into an army and I was anything but ordinary. Echo Tunnel. My father walked with me there every Sunday after I returned from church with my mother until we moved to a better place. That was the best thing he ever did for me, other than giving me a name that wouldn't let me feel ordinary for very long, no matter how persuasive the forces in my new neighborhood, my new school, in the world.

In the first place I lived, on Linn Drive in Cleveland, Ohio, we stayed in the attic of a two-family home owned by an elderly Jewish couple who lived on the first floor. There was no other place we could go at the time. I still don't know why. I remember blue walls and ceiling and thought that I lived in a box of sky. We were attic dwellers until I was four. Then the Arnsteins sold the house to the Robinsons and we moved to the second floor, real tenants. When I went back into the attic next, we were about to move, five years had passed, and there was no blue anywhere, just darkness, fraying cords, a crack where pigeons entered and molted, wooden floor planks exposed through harsh-colored linoleum. It did not look as if anyone could live there. Yet we had and it had seemed beautiful. My favorite book was *The Diary of Anne Frank;* I always thought of her as my sister and grieved the loss of her, promised never to forget her. Mr. Arnstein made an electric stove for me, and Mrs. Arnstein made a marriage certificate indicating that I was the lawful wife of Mickey Mouse. The stove still works.

By the time we moved away to Durkee Avenue, no one Jewish lived on Linn Drive. Little by little, the faces all became browner and the cooking smells in the evening were different, though they were always deep, rich smells. It was obvious the atmosphere had changed even if you drove or walked down the street and saw no one; there were different musics resounding through the brick. There were street dances and block parties. I did the shimmy and the twist. I rode a bike with a wire basket on the handlebars down the hill that ended Primrose Drive. I bought a jug of milk and fell off my bike, breaking the glass jug, cutting my leg. My mother picked out the glass, used peroxide;

I was taken to the hospital by taxi, as she was too, soon after, when she broke a green coffee cup while washing it, glass wedged deep as bone in the skin between her thumb and first finger. And though she was cut, bleeding, she still braided my hair, tied a ribbon on the ends and said how fine I looked, ribbons soaked in her blood, braids that one day caught in the stove fire I already feared and then feared more. But I did look fine, and my mother was determined to care for me no matter what disaster came along; that was important to know. Doctors removed the glass from her hand and earlier, more easily, from my leg, but she had to know for herself that not the minutest particle remained to threaten me, so she squeezed the cut every day, delayed the healing. But healing happened; there's no denying that.

Growing up, I lived in just those two places, Linn Drive and Durkee Avenue. Happiness managed to prevail no matter what happened around me, sometimes to me. That happiness is part of the freedom I found when I was in second grade, part of what I felt when my father dismantled a stinking relic in the middle of sunflowers. It is part of the power that belonged to me in Echo Tunnel. It is part of the victory I felt in the junior choir when, at eight, I led the song "Battle Hymn of the Republic," my first time leading a song. Randy Shipp, the organist I thought looked perfect for a mortician, started whispering with the organ, playing the tiniest sound so that I could be heard. I had had close to eight years listening to and admiring the preacher's voice so that when I sang "Mine eyes have seen the glory," I let loose the thunder Echo Tunnel had given me, and my child's voice filled that big church. I'm almost sure it cracked the rafters and went right out the roof like a bird, like freedom for Anne Frank and for my Easter chick that died in the attic when the attic was painted blue so we could live there better, like wings for the boy struck down by the truck, like wings for the girl who jumped out of the window, like the highest, highest note of a violin, a note I played with my voice. A note that joined the air and traveled around the world.

# ONE MORE LESSON

## Judith Ortiz Cofer

JUDITH ORTIZ COFER was born in Puerto Rico and first came to the United States at the age of four. As the daughter of a Navy man, she spent her childhood moving back and forth between Puerto Rico and New Jersey. She is now a poet and a prose writer, and has taught English and Spanish at several universities in the South. Her books of poetry include *Terms of Survival* and *Reaching for the Mainland*. Cofer is also the author of the novel, *The Line of the Sun*, and an acclaimed memoir, *Silent Dancing*, from which "One More Lesson" is taken.

"One More Lesson" revolves around her family's second move from Puerto Rico to the United States. It begins with memories of life in the small town in Puerto Rico ("the Island") where Cofer was born and ends with the family's move to an apartment in West Paterson, New Jersey.

I remember Christmas on the Island by the way it felt on my skin. The temperature dropped into the ideal seventies and even lower after midnight when some of the more devout Catholics—mostly older women—got up to go to church, *misa del gallo* they called it; mass at the hour when the rooster crowed for Christ. They would drape shawls over their heads and shoulders and move slowly toward town. The birth of Our Savior was a serious affair in our *pueblo*.

At Mamá's house, food was the focal point of *Navidad*. There were banana leaves brought in bunches by the boys, spread on the table, where the women would pour coconut candy steaming hot, and the leaves would wilt around the sticky lumps, adding an extra tang of flavor to the already irresistible treat. Someone had to watch the candy while it cooled, or it would begin to disappear as the children risked life and limb for a stolen piece of heaven. The banana leaves were also used to wrap the traditional food of holidays in Puerto Rico: *pasteles*, the meat pies made from grated yucca and plantain and stuffed with spiced meats.

Every afternoon during the week before Christmas Day, we would come home from school to find the women sitting around in the parlor with bowls on their laps, grating pieces of coconut, yuccas, plantains, cheeses—all the ingredients that would make up our Christmas Eve feast. The smells that filled Mamá's house at that time have come to mean anticipation and a sensual joy during a time in my life, the last days of my early childhood, when I could still absorb joy through my pores—when I had not yet learned that light is followed by darkness, that all of creation is based on that simple concept, and maturity is a discovery of that natural law.

It was in those days that the Americans sent baskets of fruit to our barrio—apples, oranges, grapes flown in from the States. And at night, if you dared to walk up to the hill where the mango tree stood in the dark, you could see a wonderful sight: a Christmas tree, a real pine, decorated with lights of many colors. It was the blurry outline of this tree you saw, for it was inside a screened-in porch, but we had heard a thorough description of it from the boy who delivered the fruit, a nephew of Mamá's, as it had turned out. Only I was not impressed, since just the previous year we had put up a tree ourselves in our apartment in Paterson.

Packages arrived for us in the mail from our father. I got dolls dressed in the national costumes of Spain, Italy, and Greece (at first we could not decide which of the Greek dolls was the male, since they both wore skirts); my brother got picture books; and my mother, jewelry that she would not wear, because it was too much like showing off and might attract the Evil Eye.

Evil Eye or not, the three of us were the envy of the pueblo. Everything about us set us apart, and I put away my dolls quickly when I discovered that my playmates would not be getting any gifts until *Los Reyes*—the Day of the Three Kings, when Christ received His gifts—and that even then it was more likely that the gifts they found under their beds would be practical things like clothes. Still, it was fun to find fresh grass for the camels the night the Kings were expected, tie it in bundles with string, and put it under our beds along with a bowl of fresh water.

The year went by fast after Christmas, and in the spring we received a telegram from Father. His ship had arrived in Brooklyn Yard. He gave us a date for our trip back to the States. I remember Mother's frantic packing, and the trips to Mayagüez for new clothes; the inspections of my brother's and my bodies for cuts, scrapes, mosquito bites, and other "damage" she would have to explain to Father. And I remember begging Mamá to tell me stories in the afternoons, although it was not summer yet and the trips to the mango tree had not begun. In looking back I realize that Mamá's stories were what I packed—my winter store.

Father had succeeded in finding an apartment outside Paterson's "vertical barrio," the tenement Puerto Ricans called *El Building.* He had talked a Jewish candy store owner into renting us the apartment above his establishment, which he and his wife had just vacated after buying a house in West Paterson, an affluent suburb. Mr. Schultz was a nice man whose melancholy face I was familiar with from trips I had made often with my father to his store for cigarettes. Apparently, my father had convinced him and his brother, a lookalike of Mr. Schultz who helped in the store, that we were not the usual Puerto Rican family. My father's fair skin, his ultra-correct English, and his Navy uniform were a good argument. Later it occurred to me that my father had been displaying me as a model child when he took me to that store with him. I was always dressed as if for church and held firmly by the hand. I imagine he did the same with my brother. As for my mother, her Latin beauty, her thick black hair that hung to her waist, her voluptuous body which even the winter clothes could not disguise, would have been nothing but a hindrance to my father's plans. But everyone knew that a Puerto Rican woman is her husband's satellite; she reflects both his light and his dark sides. If my father was respectable, then his family would be respectable. We got the apartment on Park Avenue.

Unlike El Building, where we had lived on our first trip to Paterson, our new home was truly in exile. There were Puerto Ricans by the hundreds only one block away, but we heard no Spanish, no loud music, no mothers yelling at children, nor the familiar *¡Ay Bendito!*, that catch-all phrase of our people. Mother lapsed into silence herself, suffering from *La Tristeza*, the sadness that only place induces and only place cures. But Father relished silence, and we were taught that silence was something to be cultivated and practiced.

Since our apartment was situated directly above where the Schultzes worked all day, our father instructed us to remove our shoes at the door and walk in our socks. We were going to prove how respectable we were by being the opposite of what our ethnic group was known to be—we would be quiet and inconspicuous.

I was escorted each day to school by my nervous mother. It was a long walk in the cooling air of fall in Paterson and we had to pass by El Building where the children poured out of the front door of the dilapidated tenement still answering their mothers in a mixture of Spanish and English: "Si, Mami, I'll come straight home from school." At the corner we were halted by the crossing guard, a strict woman who only gestured her instructions, never spoke directly to the children, and only ordered us to "halt" or "cross" while holding her white-gloved hand up at face level or swinging her arm sharply across her chest if the light was green.

The school building was not a welcoming sight for someone used to the bright colors and airiness of tropical architecture. The building looked functional. It could have been a prison, an asylum, or just what it was: an urban school for the children of immigrants, built to withstand waves of change, generation by generation. Its red brick sides rose to four solid stories. The black steel fire escapes snaked up its back like an exposed vertebra. A chain-link fence surrounded its concrete playground. Members of the elite safety patrol, older kids, sixth graders mainly, stood at each of its entrances, wearing their fluorescent white belts that criss-crossed their chests and their metal badges. No one was allowed in the building until the bell rang, not even on rainy or bitter-cold days. Only the safety patrol stayed warm.

My mother stood in front of the main entrance with me and a growing crowd of noisy children. She looked like one of us, being no taller than the six-grade girls. She held my hand so tightly that my fingers cramped. When the bell rang, she walked me into the building and kissed my cheek. Apparently my father had done all the paperwork for my enrollment, because the next thing I remember was being led to my third-grade classroom by a black girl who had emerged from the principal's office.

Though I had learned some English at home during my first years in Paterson, I had let it recede deep into my memory while learning Spanish in Puerto Rico. Once again I was the child in the cloud of silence, the one who had to be spoken to in sign language as if she were a deaf-mute. Some of the children even raised their voices when they spoke to me, as if I had trouble hearing. Since it was a large troublesome class composed mainly of black and Puerto Rican children, with a few working-class Italian children interspersed, the teacher paid little attention to me. I re-learned the language quickly by the immersion method. I remember one day, soon after I joined the rowdy class, when our regular teacher was absent and Mrs. D., the sixth-grade teacher from across the hall, attempted to monitor both classes. She scribbled something on the chalkboard and went to her own room. I felt a pressing need to use the bathroom and asked Julio, the Puerto Rican boy who sat behind me, what I had to do to be excused. He said that Mrs. D. had written on the board that we could be excused by simply writing our names under the sign. I got up from my desk and started for the front of the room when I was struck on the head hard with a book. Startled and hurt, I turned around expecting to find one of the bad boys in my class, but it was Mrs. D. I faced. I remember her angry face, her fingers on my arms pulling me back to my desk, and her voice saying incomprehensible things to me in a hissing tone. Someone finally explained to her that I was new, that I did not speak English. I also remember how suddenly her face changed from anger to anxiety. But I did not forgive her for hitting me with that hard-cover spelling book. Yes, I would recognize that book even now. It was not until years later that I stopped hating that teacher for not understanding that I had been betrayed by a classmate, and by my inability to read her warning on the board. I instinctively understood then that language is the only weapon a child has against the absolute power of adults.

I quickly built up my arsenal of words by becoming an insatiable reader of books.

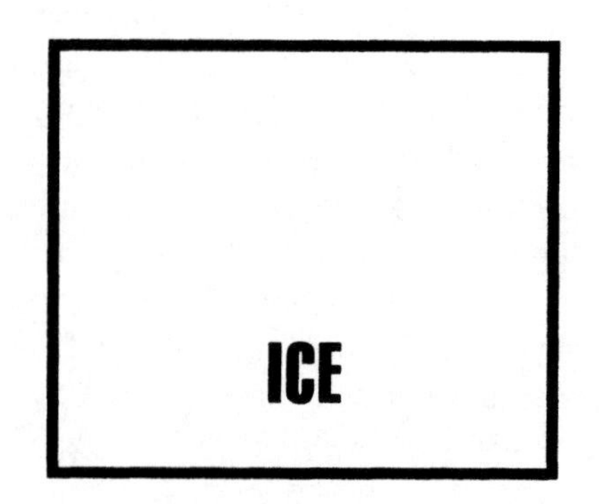

# ICE

## Graham Salisbury

GRAHAM SALISBURY, a descendant of New Engalnd missionaries, grew up on the islands of Oahu and Hawaii. He has worked as a deep-sea charter fishing boat deck hand, a glass-bottom-boat skipper, a musician, a graphic artist, and an elementary school teacher. Today he writes novels and stories, and manages an historic office building in Portland, Oregon, where he lives with his family. He is the author of two novels, the award-winning *Blue Skin of the Sea* and *Under the Blood-Red Sun*.

I got into my share of fights as a kid. I was short. And white.

People called me shrimp, shahkbait, mongoose, pip-squeak, runt, hanakuso, half-pint, cock-a-roach, zit, and a lot of other more gross and disgusting things. That was okay when it was coming from my friends. I was a haole boy. A minority. Fair game. My roots in the Hawaiian Islands went back to 1820, which meant exactly zero. But I was one of the boys. They liked me and I liked them. Race wasn't an issue. But coolness was, and I was cool enough. I could take whatever they dished out. I knew they were just doing their job. Besides, I called them worse things back. And we all laughed about it.

But sometimes boys who weren't my friends called me things I didn't want to be called. Like futface, *she-she* pants, or sissy.

*Bok!* Nobody was calling me a sissy. *Bok! Bok!*

I even fractured my finger once, throwing a punch that missed and hit the school bus window. Hurt like fire for days, and I was sorry I'd gotten into that fight.

Even so, I believed it was good to be a fighter. It was healthy. Got stuff out of my system. I still believe it's good. But I've long since learned that you don't have to fight with your fists to be a fighter. In fact, it's better not to.

My problem was I never asked myself what *kind* of fighter I was. I never even thought about it, and I should have. But for much of my youth, thinking wasn't a primary character trait. I just did it—whatever it was—then paid the price. I should have thought about *why* I got into fights. Was I fighting for myself, or was I just trying to prove something to someone else? There's a difference, you know. A big difference. I learned that the hard way, mostly by fighting stupid fights.

But I learned it best from a block of ice.

I had three fathers, none of whom I knew.

My real father was a fighter pilot in the U.S. Navy. Lt. Commander Henry Forester Graham, VBF 83, USS *Essex*. He went down with his plane on my first birthday. The exact day. April eleventh. He was only twenty-seven years old. I never knew him, except through letters my mother received from his fellow officers after his death, letters which mostly said: "I only hope the boy grows up to be half the man Hank Graham was."

A year or so later my mother married another navy man, Guy Salisbury, who adopted me. He lived with us eight years, fathered my three sisters, then died of cancer at the age of thirty-three. He was a "sweetheart and a fine, fine man, just like your father was," my aunt told me. He was also a busy man, and I hardly ever saw him.

I didn't know him either, but at least I can remember what he looked like.

Two or three years after that my mother married again. A beachboy. A man named John, who was ten years younger than she was. He had thick, wavy hair and muscles like Sylvester

Stallone. He could surf, he could water-ski on bare feet, he could free-dive to eighty feet and stay down for close to three minutes. He was once stranded on French Frigate Shoals for thirty days with a couple of Filipino fishermen. And except for one, gaping character flaw, he was everything I, at thirteen, wanted to be.

His flaw, though, was a big one, and I didn't understand it until I was much older. But once I figured it out, I could see why I never knew him, either.

It simply wasn't possible.

He wouldn't allow it.

He was a loner and a crusher of self-esteem—mine, and my sisters', and eventually my mother's. But for a few years in my life, John was king. He was lean and strong, and he looked like a movie star. In my eyes he could do no wrong. My sisters never saw it that way, but I sure did. I liked him. I was floating on top of the world when Mom said she was going to marry him.

We lived on Oahu at the time. John worked at the Hawaiian Village Hotel in Waikiki, running the water-ski operation. He was then, and had always been, a man of the sea. His skin was a deep red-brown, colored by a lifetime in the sun. And when he moved, it was in a smooth, slow, don't-bother-me kind of way. Most of the time a Marlboro hung from his half-parted lips, his eyes squinting through the smoke like Clint Eastwood's. He could have been the star of *Sea Hunt*, or *Rawhide*, or even *Cliffhanger*, if he wanted to. He had that same kind of raw, manly presence.

We moved from Oahu to the Big Island soon after Mom and John were married. We traveled by boat—a thirty-eight-foot deep-sea charter fishing boat that made me sicker than I'd ever been in my life. My sisters took a plane. But Mom and I made the two-day trip with John and his new fully rigged haole sampan, gliding over glassy seas in the lee of the islands and battering through the channels between them, channels that threw the boat around like a cork in a hurricane. John was in heaven. My mother was oblivious, a newlywed caught up in the Big Bopper singing "Chantilly Lace" on the boat's radio. I was sickly green, dehydrated, and barely human.

Two days later we cruised into Kailua-Kona in the calm lee of Mount Hualalai. There, in the shade of groves of coconut trees that lined the shore, was my new home, a serene, turquoise-bayed fishing village where John was going to be a charter-boat skipper. The sun was more brilliant there than in any other place I'd ever been. It made the glassy water in the harbor sparkle. And it warmed the vast, mysterious ocean that relentlessly hissed along the shoreline, an ocean that reached out and put its arms around you, called you closer, like the sirens in *The Odyssey*. You could have called it paradise, because it just about was. And there I stood on the pier, the heir apparent to all of John's great wealth of maritime knowledge.

Day after day I followed him around, watching, mimicking. I walked like John. I scowled like John. I made John remarks to my sisters, terse and scornful and sarcastic. I carried my T-shirt hanging from the back pocket of my shorts and squinted into the sun like I'd been on the ocean all my life.

At home, John did a multitude of secret things in the garage. But mostly he made lures out of fiberglass resin. Plugs, he called them. Tubular-shaped things about the size of the cardboard center of a roll of toilet paper. He'd put plastic eyes and pearl inlays into his mold. Then, when they'd dried, he'd fit them with flashy plastic and rubber skirts that wiggled in the water. Finally he'd drill a hole down the center and thread through a wire leader and a hook big enough to handle a thousand-pound marlin. He made plugs in every color combination he could think of, trying to find the prize among them, the one that would *work*, the one that would catch the Big Fish.

On a technical level, I was privy to none of this. I could only watch from a distance, could not touch anything, could not even ask a question. The one time I did, his answer was vague and totally useless. Fishermen, it seemed, guarded their secrets even from the ignorant.

Still, I watched him, like a cat watches a dove peck around in the grass.

My mother practically begged him to let me work as his deck hand. John scowled and told her I was too small. He needed someone with muscle, and brains. But Mom persisted. Maybe she was worried that John was right and hoped that a summer on the boat would shape me up.

In the end, her wish was granted. I got the job. I was a deck hand on a deep-sea charter fishing boat, the youngest and smallest in the Kona fleet. All the other skippers and their first-rate deck hands were kind and supportive, always smiled and waved at me from the decks of their boats. One of them even told me I looked like a miniature Tarzan, which I loved to hear, because John looked like Tarzan.

The major part of my job, I soon found out, took place between getting up in the morning and heading out to sea three hours later. Then, for the next eight hours, I did little more than go for a boat ride . . . unless we caught a fish. Then I sat at the wheel and tried to keep the angler's line behind the boat. I was a spectator. Because that's when the muscle came in, and the brains . . . which, of course, I didn't have. John reminded me of the void between my ears almost daily, in all sorts of unspoken ways.

But who cared? I was working. On a boat. We caught *big* fish—up to a thousand pounds, sometimes. And we took out famous people, like Red Skelton, Spencer Tracy, and a football player named Paul Hornung, the biggest human being I'd ever seen in my life. How many other fourteen-year-old boys could say that?

I was to work an entire summer with John. That was the deal Mom had made for me. The first week I did nothing but handle the wharf lines, tying and untying the boat at the pier. Then I got to sponge the salt from the seats and windows at the beginning and end of each day. That, I began to realize, was all I was going to get. John was accommodating my mother, not training a deck hand.

Wanting to prove that I was good enough, and hoping to gain a small shot of approval from John, I dreamed up a set of duties for myself. I figured I could start by doing more to get the boat ready in the mornings.

I studied John's routine until it was as clear as the resin

in his prize lures: the night before, check the two-gallon bucket of water in the freezer in the garage; get up at five in the morning and take the bucket out of the freezer and work the ice out, then put the ice on a burlap bag on the back seat of the Jeep; refill the bucket and put it back in the freezer; take a couple of six-packs of Coke and Budweiser from the storage closet and set them next to the ice; unscrew the five-horse Evinrude outboard engine from its sawhorse stand and throw it in the Jeep, too; drive to the harbor in silence; take the ice out of the Jeep and put it on your hand, like a waiter carrying a tray of dishes; grab the outboard with the other hand and walk slowly down to the skiff; set the outboard on the back of the skiff, fire it up, and buzz on out into the harbor to get the boat.

This was what John did, day after day. It seemed simple enough. I could do all of that. All he'd have to do was have a first cup of coffee from his corroding silver Thermos.

I asked him if I could take over the job of the ice and the outboard.

John studied me a moment, smoke drifting off the end of his cigarette. Then he shrugged, and said, "I don't care." That's all he had to say about it, nothing more, nothing less.

*Yes!* I thought. I'll do it just like he did it. When I get that down, he'll ask me to do more. He'll see that I can be a good deck hand, that I have muscles and brains.

That night, I checked to be sure the water in the bucket was freezing up. Even got the drinks and put them in the garage near the outboard. Easy. No sweat.

John banged on my bedroom door at five the next morning, just like always. Boom! One time. That's all. No words. I heard it or I didn't. If I didn't, he'd leave me behind without a second thought. I got up instantly, a habit I developed then, and cling to even to this day.

I couldn't get the ice out of the bucket. I kicked it, I twisted it, I pounded it on the ground, I swore at it, but it wouldn't budge. John suddenly appeared at my side and pushed me out of the way. Without saying a word, he took an ice pick and chiseled an inch of ice off the top, all the way around, leaving a space between the lip of the bucket and the block of ice. Then he turned the bucket over and dropped it on the ground.

The ice popped out.

You needed to leave a drop-space around the top of the bucket. Simple. Part of where the brains came in. John hadn't told me that, and I hadn't noticed. He picked up the ice and put it in the Jeep. Then the Evinrude and the drinks. When we got to the pier, he took both the ice and the engine down to the skiff himself.

The next day I did it right, got the ice out of the bucket and put it in the Jeep. Then the outboard engine. It was heavy. I wasn't sure I could carry both of them at the same time.

On the way to the pier, I decided I would only take the ice, at least until I could do that much without screwing up. I told that to John when we got there. He shook his head and grabbed the engine and started walking toward the skiff. No words had passed his lips since the night before, when he told me to do the ice right this time.

I took the ice off the back seat and, as John always did, raised it to my shoulder on the palm of my hand. I started following him, walking slowly, in the don't-bother-me way, which I had mastered. It wasn't far, maybe thirty or forty yards. When we got about halfway, my hand started feeling like it was on fire. It froze so badly it burned. I had to switch hands. I ended up carrying the ice cradled between both arms, nestled against my chest. When we got to the skiff, I dropped the ice down onto the floorboards and jammed my hands into the warm ocean, and let them sting until I could move my fingers again.

John fired up the outboard and started out into the harbor to the boat, silent and sullen as a flat tire.

I spent the next eight hours being angry at myself, wondering how I was ever going to carry that blasted ice *and* the outboard from the Jeep to the skiff at the same time.

The ice was just too cold to carry in one hand that far, at John's impossibly slow pace. I didn't know how he could do it, except that his hands were thick and leathery from fishing all his life. Mine were lily-white and as soft as raw fish meat. Once, the ice burned me so badly that I had to set it down on the hood of a truck . . . just for a second . . . while I buried my hands in my armpits.

John stopped, and looked back at me, and said, "Tsk . . ."

And I knew I was losing ground.

After a couple of weeks of murdering my screaming hands, I came up with a solution. I put a canvas fish glove on . . . *then* carried the stupid ice. It worked. So simple, and well worth the scorn I figured John would pour all over me for being so sissy as to have to put on a glove.

But he didn't say a word about it.

Not one word.

In fact, I don't think he even noticed. I was trying so hard to be like him, trying to live up to this self-imposed manly goal of carrying ice with my bare hand, when the reality of it all suddenly hit me—*who cared?*

Certainly not John. He didn't give a rat's you-know-what how I carried the ice, just as long as I got it to the boat.

Only I cared.

Why?

Because I didn't know any better. Because I was fighting for the wrong reason. I was being watched. Right? I was being watched by John, and all the other fishermen, and all their ace deck hands, and all the kids on shore who were rubbing their hands together to have my job if I couldn't do it. I *had* to live up to the code, the image, the machismo. I had no choice in the matter. Right?

Wasn't that right?

Carrying ice taught me a great lesson, though I didn't truly understand it until years later. But there it was, right in front of me, and I didn't see it. I *still* tried to carry the ice bare-handed a couple of times, and *still* failed. And I still felt as if I'd never live up to John's expectations.

I kicked myself around for a long time before I finally realized that John didn't *have* any expectations. He didn't seem to care much what I did, one way or the other.

Today, I thank John for letting me work on his boat. And

I thank him for being the way he was. I learned a lot simply by being there. He truly was a wealth of knowledge. But most of all, I learned about how hard I tried, even into later years, to please *others* rather than myself, always searching for that elusive outside approval. Long, hard, bumbling years dragged by before I finally understood how foolish, if not impossible, that search was.

Jeeze. To think back. How I would do all manner of stupid things in order to be accepted, to be seen as manly. Nobody was calling *me* a sissy, confonnit.

And nobody's calling *you* one, either. Right?

You're going with the bare hand. Grit it out until your fingers fall off.

Good. I understand that. You're a fighter. You gotta do what you gotta do.

But just one thing. Are you doing it for you? Or are you doing it for someone else? It's an important question.

# MATH AND AFTER MATH

## Lensey Namioka

LENSEY NAMIOKA was born in Beijing, China. She moved with her family to the United States when she was nine years old. She has lived in various parts of the country, including New England, New York, and California. She and her husband now live in Seattle, Washington.

Namioka has published numerous books, including *The Samurai and the Long-Nosed Devils* (set in Japan, her husband's country), *Who's Hu?*, *Yang the Youngest and His Terrible Ear*, *Yang the Third and Her Impossible Family*, and *April and the Dragon Lady*. Besides writing, Lensey Namioka's favorite activities include cooking, traveling, going to the movies and playing the piano. Her husband is a professor of mathematics at the University of Washington, and they have two daughters.

"Seven!" shouted the teacher.

Or did he shout "Four"?

I shrank down in my seat. Math class was an absolute nightmare. The teacher scared me so much that my hands got sweaty, and my fingers slipped on the abacus beads.

I was in the second grade when I discovered that I suffered from abacus anxiety. The trouble was that I was going to a school where the teacher spoke a different dialect. I grew up with Mandarin, the dialect spoken by the majority of the Chinese. When the eastern part of China was occupied by the Japanese, our family moved inland, to a region where I could barely understand the local dialect.

Writing was the pretty much the same in any dialect, so in language and history classes I didn't have trouble with what was on the blackboard. My problems started in the math class, where we had to learn the abacus. Before the days of the calculator, the abacus was the main tool for adding and multiplying. It still is, in many parts of China (as well as in countries like Japan and Russia).

The abacus teacher would shout out the numbers he wanted us to add or multiply. My ears didn't always understand what he said, so *seven*, for instance, sounded a lot like *four*.

Until that class, math was one of my better subjects, especially when it came to multiplication. Years later, when we emigrated to America, I was astounded to hear one of my American friends recite the multiplication table:

"Two times one is two. Two times two is four. Two times three is six . . ." It seemed to take forever.

The multiplication table is much shorter in Chinese. One reason is that the Chinese names for numbers are all one-syllable. We don't have numbers like *seven*.

Also, we omit words like *times* and *equals* while reciting. Instead of "Seven times two equals fourteen," we say, *Er qi shi si*, or literally, *two seven fourteen*. So we do it in four syllables instead of eight.

The best trick is that we memorize only half as many entries, because we know that seven times two is the same as two times seven. (I learned later this was called the Commutative Law).

This meant I could rattle off the multiplication table about three times faster than my American classmates. But I learned the table even faster than my *Chinese* classmates. The reason was that I sang it.

"You can remember a tune better than a string of numbers," my father told me. "So I want you to sing the multiplication table."

The standard way to teach musical notation in Chinese schools was to give numbers to the diatonic scale: *do* was one (not a female deer), *re* was two (not a ray of sunshine), *mi* was three, and so o When I had to remember that two times seven was fourteen, my father told me to hum the little tune *re ti do fa*. This was not a pretty tune, but it certainly stuck in my mind.

Following Father's suggestion, I learned the multiplication table very quickly, and even now I still hum. The other day, when I was in the store buying candy bars, I noticed another customer staring at me. I was trying to figure out if my fistful of change was enough for four candy bars, and I must have been humming as I multiplied.

When I entered American schools, my best subject was math. I didn't need to know much English to manage the Arabic numbers, and my Chinese school had been a year ahead of American schools in math (because of shorter multiplication tables, maybe).

After a while I realized that my classmates found me weird. During our early years in America, my family lived in towns where there weren't too many Asians, and I looked different from everybody else in class. It turned out that my weirdness wasn't just because I looked different, or because I hummed funny tunes.

"How come you're so good at math?" asked one of my classmates.

"Why shouldn't I be?" I asked.

"You're a girl!"

In America, apparently, it was unusual for a girl to be good at math. It was different in China, where women were good at figures. They regularly kept the household accounts and managed the family budget.

A few years ago, I saw a movie about Chinese-Americans called *Dim Sum*. A Chinese man who ran a restaurant in Chinatown brought his receipts to a woman friend, who figured out his accounts for him.

My American friends found the situation strange. "It's not unusual at all," I told them. "In my family, for instance, my mother made the major financial decisions."

In fact, my mother made a financial killing when we were living in Berkeley, California. A neighbor took her to a land auction. A piece of land near our house was offered for sale, and Mother thought it would be fun to bid on it. Someone was bound to top her bid, she thought.

She was stunned when nobody else made a bid, and Mother found herself the owner of a large plot of land.

As she and her friend prepared to leave the auction room, a man rushed up to them. He was a realtor who had planned to bid for the land, but had arrived at the auction too late.

"I'll give you whatever you paid, plus something extra!" he told Mother.

"No, thank you," said Mother. "I'm quite happy with the purchase."

The realtor raised his offer, but Mother still turned him down. He became frantic. "Look, I'll go as high as two thousand dollars above your bid!"

This just made Mother more stubborn. "No, I want to keep the land."

The realtor obtained our address and phone number, and immediately called our house.

When Father answered the phone, the realtor shouted, "Do you know what your wife just did? She threw away a chance to make two thousand dollars!"

"I'm sure she had her reasons," Father answered calmly. Nothing that the realtor said could disturb him.

The land turned out to be an excellent investment, and helped to provide a tidy nest egg for my parents in their old age.

In many other Asian countries, too, the housewife is the one who manages money. It's normal for the husband to hand over his paycheck to his wife, and out of it she gives him an allowance. Perhaps it's the result of Confucius's teaching that a gentleman is above money, so it's the woman's duty to be concerned with such petty matters.

Things were very different in America. An American husband would hit the roof if his wife did what my mother had done. Women here were supposed to be hopeless when it came to money matters and figures.

Many girls got good math grades in elementary school,

but their grades began to slip when they entered middle school. By then they were getting interested in boys, and they didn't want the boys to think they were weird.

I was weird in elementary and middle school because I was a real whiz at multiplication. In high school, I continued to be a whiz in my geometry and algebra classes. I was lucky to have a geometry teacher who addressed us by last name and didn't care whether you were a boy or a girl, as long as you agreed with Euclid.

My high school geometry class was also the first place where the word *argument* meant something good. My parents complained that I was always arguing. In geometry class, making an argument meant presenting something in an orderly, logical manner.

I also liked story or word problems in my algebra class. Years later, when I was teaching math, I couldn't understand why many students complained bitterly about them. To me, story problems meant fiction, romance. The most exciting one involved an army column marching forward at a certain speed. A messenger at the head of the column was sent back to the rear. If the column was so many miles long, would he be able to deliver his message in time? I pictured the following scenario:

"We expect to engage the enemy in half an hour," the commander told the messenger. "You have to get word to the men in the rear of the column!"

The mud-splashed rider desperately lashed his horse, while arrows fell on him from ambushers. How fast did he have to ride so that he would reach the rear guard in time to deliver his message?

Attacking these story problems with relish, I was usually one of the first in the class to finish, and I was often sent to the board to write out the solution.

By the time I started college, I began to realize that it was unusual, unnatural—maybe even unhealthy—for girls to be good at math. I entered Radcliffe College, which was connected with Harvard. Some of my laboratory courses were taken together with the Harvard students, but classes such as English and math were taught separately on the small Radcliffe campus.

The English classes usually had around twenty students, but my beginning calculus class had only five of us. According to rumor, new instructors at Harvard were assigned to teach Radcliffe math classes as a test.

"If they manage to get through the year without breaking down, they're allowed to go on to higher things," we heard.

On the first day of our math class, the instructor (who later became a famous mathematician) crept into the room without looking at us, and spent the whole period mumbling into the blackboard. In fact, he spent the whole year mumbling into the blackboard.

"He's awfully shy, isn't he?" I remarked to a friend.

"Maybe he's just scared of girls who study math," she said.

Things got better when I entered the University of California, which was co-ed. The math classes were larger, and five girls in a class of forty boys weren't enough to scare the instructors.

By this time I knew that in America a girl who was good at math was not only unusual, unnatural, unhealthy, but—worst of all—unattractive.

"Boys don't date you if you're a math whiz," I was told.

The situation was different for me. First of all, racial cross-dating was still rare when I was in college, so I dated only Chinese-American boys, who were hardened to the sight of their mothers or sisters doing math.

I got very good grades in math throughout my school years and majored in mathematics in college. I had a head start in the multiplication table, and I loved arguing and proving things. By the time I learned that I wasn't supposed to do well in math, it was too late.

A hot topic when I was in graduate school was the right-brain, left-brain debate. Scientists decided that men tended to use their left brain, which was the reasoning part, while women used their right brain, the intuitive part.

"That's why we're good at hard sciences and math," the boys in my classes assured us. "You girls should stick with poetry, history, art, and things like that. It's a matter of genes or hormones."

Then, later studies showed that the Japanese listened to insect sounds with their left (analytic) brain, while Westerners listened to insects with their right brain. Still other studies showed that professional musicians (both male and female) listened to music with the analytic side of their brain, while the general public listened with their intuitive side.

It began to seem that training and social pressure, not genes and hormones, influenced which side of the brain was used. I eagerly followed the debate and could hardly wait for the day when it was okay for women to study science and math in America.

Today, attitudes are finally beginning to change. My daughters tell me that girls in high school math classes are less afraid to do well, and many women go into science and math in college. (One of my daughters is a computer scientist, and the other is an engineer.)

For years, I seemed to be doing well in math because of my Chinese background, because I wasn't afraid to get good math grades in school. I did all the assigned problems without much trouble. But it wasn't enough to do all the problems assigned by the teacher. To be a creative mathematician, you also have to make up problems. I finally learned that I would never do really original work in mathematics.

I found that, for math at least, I lacked what the Chinese call *huo qi*, literally "fiery breath," in other words, ambition and drive. In English the expression "fire in the belly" comes close. I didn't think I was creative enough in mathematics to do good research, nor did I have the drive.

My immediate excuse for getting out of math was the difficulty of arranging for childcare. To be completely honest, I have to admit that I left mathematics because I wasn't all that good, despite my early impressive grades.

I made the transition from mathematics to freelance writing through translation work. For a brief period, I translated mathematical papers from Chinese into English.

My work dried up, however, when the Cultural Revolution

swept over China. Mathematicians, like other scholars, were ordered to stop research and write papers confessing their political shortcomings. (These were the lucky ones. The unlucky ones spent their time cleaning latrines.) With no mathematical papers to translate, I eventually took up freelance writing.

My parents reproached me. "How can you give up a beautiful subject like mathematics?"

"We can admire beautiful pictures or music," I told them. "But we don't all have the gift to paint or compose."

"You spent so many years studying math," some people say. "Does it help you at all in your writing?"

Math has taught me the useful lesson of thrift. I've met hundreds of mathematicians, and not one of them was a spendthrift. In math you're taught to squeeze the strongest possible result out of the weakest possible hypothesis—in other words, you try to get the most value for your money.

This thrifty habit stayed with me after I became a writer. When I put people or events into a book, I squeeze the most out of them. Very few things are thrown in and then forgotten later. As a result my plots seem to be carefully worked out in advance, instead of being made up as I go along.

Years ago, I enjoyed story problems because the stories fired my imagination. In fact, writing fiction was where I finally found my "fiery breath." Instead of story problems, I can write problem stories. And that's what I'm still doing today.

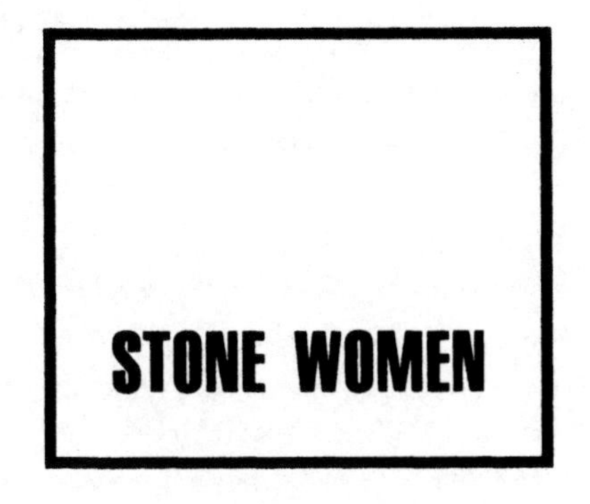

# STONE WOMEN

## Susan Power

SUSAN POWER is a member of the Standing Rock Sioux tribe. She grew up in Chicago; earned degrees from Harvard/Radcliffe, Harvard Law School, and the University of Iowa Writers' Workshop; and is the author of *The Grass Dancer*, a novel. She writes, "At the University of Iowa, I took a class on Autobiography. The final assignment was to write the first chapter of my own autobiography, resulting in 'Stone Women.' I was struck by the fact that I was not the main presence in this chapter, but was rather shadowed by older relatives, even ancestors I have never met. Those who came before me have had an impact on my personal experience. My mother told me their stories, reminded me that I am not in this life alone but am connected to all kinds of people. History is very much alive for me."

My grandfather is hiding in a hole. His wife and eldest five children used spoons, tin cups and copper pans to dig a hole near the stove in their two-bedroom cabin. It is lucky they have a dirt floor so my grandfather can crouch in a hole under the kitchen table.

My mother, Susan, and her sister Elsie find magazines for him to read in the shadows. Magazines are hard to find. I think the reservation priest lends them *National Geographic*. Susan and Elsie walk through town looking for cigarette butts. Later, at home, they will make cigarettes for my grandfather to smoke under the kitchen table. My mother likes to watch the smoke rising mysteriously from the ground, winding between the ankles of seated children. Whenever a visitor stops by, the children warn their father and he must pinch the end of his cigarette and close his magazine.

I imagine he closes his eyes and listens to the houseguest. Will it be the police? Will they find him? Will they insult his wife and embarrass his children? I wonder whether he regrets his taste for liquor, so strong that he will drink rubbing alcohol or vanilla extract. It is 1935 and against the law for Indians to purchase or drink alcohol even though Prohibition has ended. The laws won't change for twenty years.

My grandfather speaks old-time Dakota but looks more like a white man than any of his drinking buddies, so he can buy them all liquor once in a while. But someone has told on him and the police are searching, waiting for him to surface as they know he will when the urge to drink gets too strong.

I want to know what my grandfather is thinking. Does he speak English or Dakota in his mind? He rubs the stump of his left leg in the dark, the damp earth makes it ache more than usual. He must remember running away from Indian boarding school when he touches it. Perhaps he is just as frightened now as he was at age eleven when his sweaty hands couldn't keep a firm grip on the boxcar ladder and he fell beneath the train.

I want to sew him a Ghost Dance shirt. I want to use the softest buckskin and brightest paints. I will paint the history of our family on its front and back with such careful strokes everyone will say it is a miracle: Look, she has included our ancestors' vision of the coming intruder; she has included our move from the East to the West; there are the battles of White Stone Hill and Little Big Horn; there are our dead chiefs—Gall, Sitting Bull, Crazy Horse, Two Bears; there is the White Buffalo Calf Woman and her gift of the sacred pipe; there is Wounded Knee and the mass graves; there are our boys in World War I; there is her grandfather slipping under the train.

I will sew tassels of horse hair and medicine wheels made of dyed porcupine quills on the shirt. I will trim its edges with long glass bugle beads so my grandfather sparkles in the sun.

The Ghost Dance shirt will make him invisible to whites so he can move through this country like a man on a bold vision quest. The Ghost Dance shirt will heal his leg and cure his taste for liquor. He will be the tallest man in Fort Yates, North Dakota, on the Standing Rock Sioux Reservation. He will whisper my Dakota name, Wákča Waštéwi, as he walks along the Grand River, counting the water moccasins he sees resting on its shore, and he will smile, knowing that I am coming.

My mother was born in 1925 on the Standing Rock Sioux Reservation which extends into both North and South Dakota. Her parents were Yanktonnai Sioux (Dakota), and her great-grandfather was Chief Mató Nupá (Two Bears), who lead the Battle of White Stone Hill in 1863 and eventually became a Catholic convert.

"We should never have converted," my mother tells me, "that's the start of all our problems. We ticked off our ancestors by doing that, so now they won't help us."

But I imagine Two Bears must be doing his best, helping me get good grades, moving my pen when it is heavy and the paper is silent, helping my husband when he operates on patients, helping my mother when she feels the pain of the world. Two Bears is trying to make amends for being taken in by that traveling priest, Father DeSmet.

The log cabin where my mother lived as a child burned down long ago but she has taken me to its location. We can't walk near the foundation or scratch in the dirt of the old yard because it is ten feet underwater, flooded by the government's construction of the Oahe Dam.

"Goddamn that Oahe Dam!" my mother says. "This reservation was so little land to begin with, and now a good portion of it is underwater. Useless. That dam is greedy."

I dream that the Oahe Dam has a wide mouth and chunky teeth, its lips rasp like paper as it eats our reservation. I tell it to stop, stop, and it laughs, opening its mouth the way children do to be naughty. I see long grass and dirt lining its throat, and the bones of my ancestors caught in its teeth. The snap of its closing mouth wakes me up and I realize the sound is my mother, unpinning her hair and dropping bobby pins into an old Vaseline jar.

My mother takes me to see the Stone Woman and I am disappointed. Standing Rock is named after her; her figure rests on a brick pedestal outside the Indian Agency office in Fort Yates. She is so much smaller than I'd imagined.

My mother traces a finger over the rock to point out her features. "This is her face. You see how she's hiding it under her shawl? And this is the baby strapped to her back."

I reach up my hand to pat the baby's back. My mother tells me the story of the Stone Woman as we stand beside her. I have heard the legend so often it can't be for my benefit. Perhaps my mother is scolding this ancestor-sister.

"Here she is, this pouting woman. You see how she is hunched and looking at the ground? They say she was always moody and a little spoiled. She was so beautiful, she was used to people admiring her and letting her get her own way.

"I believe she loved her husband as much as she could love anyone. But I don't think she was a very good wife. So her husband found a second wife with a sweeter disposition. He picked her out just before they took down the village to move to winter camp. This woman didn't move a finger to help. The second wife did all the work, took down the lodge poles herself and folded the skins. Everyone was set to go but this woman wouldn't budge. She sat on the ground, her shawl over her head, practically smothering the baby on her back. Her husband begged and threatened, tried everything to get her on her feet. But she pouted. She was good at that. They left her there, figuring she would follow eventually. The next day she still hadn't turned up so her husband and his brother went back to find her. They found her sure enough. Turned to stone, and the baby with her. That's what pouting will get you."

I rub the child's back a little more before leaving. The

baby is the most tragic part of the story for me. I want to hold its heavy little body and hug it against me until it is warm.

My mother was the third of eight children, four girls and four boys. She was closest to Elsie who was less than a year older. People thought they looked like twins.

"I was always the responsible one," my mother complains, "even though Helen and Elsie were older. I made the boys mind and kept the place clean for Mama. I learned to cook nearly as soon as I learned to walk."

Elsie was the mischief-maker and my mother was her timid accomplice. It was Elsie who wanted to know if she could still hear the tick of a buried clock. Elsie and mother went to the Lugers' store in town where Elsie swiped a clock.

"I'll put it back when I'm through," she reassured her sister.

They buried the clock behind their cabin in a hole only one or two feet deep. "We could still hear that clock," my mother tells me. "The dirt didn't mess up the works. But it sounded more like a heartbeat than a clock."

My grandmother caught them and was furious, making them return the clock. But it is significant to me that my mother heard its heart beating in the ground because it is just like her. If there is magic, my mother will find it. If there are spirits, my mother will see them. My mother leaves the cleanest bones on her plate after a meal. The bones are usually cracked because she has eaten the marrow which she says is so tasty. She tells me it is because she was a Dust Bowl Depression child, but I am skeptical. When I see those little white bones I know it is just the way my mother lives her life.

My mother is a genius, at least I have always thought it was quite clever of her to teach herself to read when she was three years old. The only book the family owned was on child labor, and my mother was desperate to learn the stories behind the sad faces in photographs.

"It was the first time I felt close to white children. I looked at their faces and knew what they were thinking,'' she says. She read that book so many times she memorized it, and can still quote passages and statistics in a rhythmic voice that fashions the text into a poem. Sometimes she would sit by Sitting Bull's grave and recite for him. "We used to put his poor old ghost through hell,'' she tells me.

Sitting Bull was originally buried across the road from my mother's cabin. Later, white businessmen would dig him up and cart him away to Mobridge, South Dakota, hoping to attract tourist dollars. But when my mother was little, he was a benevolent presence. Children called on him to intercede with angry parents, and prayed to him the way they prayed to saints when the nuns stood over them in church.

A few lonely tourists would straggle onto the reservation to visit his grave, and when they did, my mother and the other children would pretend they couldn't speak English so the tourists would take their pictures and talk about them openly. With smiling faces, Elsie and my mother would curse them in Dakota, using their hands to signal "Drop Dead'' in Indian Sign Language.

"You were bad,'' I tell her.

"We were bad,'' she admits with a smile.

I feel left out when my mother describes spectral visits.

"My father's mother came to say goodbye to me,'' she whispers, showing me a picture of a woman who looks like my mother in a long dress. "She died hundreds of miles away but her spirit came to me in the night. She watched me from the foot of the bed I shared with Helen, Elsie, and Margaret. You know Helen, she can sleep through anything. When she got up to go to the outhouse she walked right through Grandma and didn't even notice. That's when I knew Grandma was dead.''

"Weren't you scared?'' I have asked her. Someday I expect her to say yes.

"No. She was always good to me. She had the sweetest smile. Why should I be afraid?''

I am afraid. I am afraid for her in the big bed, sleeping

under the frost-lined ceiling. I am afraid the grandmother will reach for her and take her away, somewhere she will have to stay so she will never meet my father. I am afraid I won't be born. I am afraid my own dead grandmothers will look for me, lonely in the afterlife which might be boring. They always liked to hear me sing and tell stories. I am also afraid they will never come. I will never see them again. They will never love me enough to push across the border that has separated us for so long.

So much fear, my mother would say. I think she would be disgusted. It is the white side coming out, she would accuse me if she knew. Only she would use the Dakota word, *wašíčun*, to make me feel doubly ashamed. So I listen to her story and accept that she has no fear. I have enough for us both.

My mother tells me about Indian boarding school. She covers her eyes with her hand.

Elsie and my mother were holding hands, attached to a line of Indian girls strung out across the hospital corridor. Sister Michael stood facing them, her round face pinched red by a wimple.

*She has unhappy flesh*, my mother was thinking.

The girls' faces were impassive except for Elsie's, her nostrils flared as they always did when she was annoyed. Sister Michael would probably beat her for it later but she didn't care. Elsie was tough.

Sister Michael had brought them to the maternity ward so they would understand the consequences of sin. The girls heard women crying, sometimes screaming, which seemed to please their teacher.

"Listen carefully," she told them. "Listen even if it is difficult. This is the Pain Our Dear Lord visited on Eve for giving in to temptation. This is the curse that we carry throughout life as her descendants. This is the Lord's judgment."

"This is cheslí," *crap*, Elsie whispered to my mother. My mother smiled and Sister Michael was quick to confront the sisters.

"You'll be the first in hell," she declared, pointing at

Elsie, "but it will be hell on earth, too. You're heading right into the Pain. You keep it up, keep being smart. You'll be sorry."

Sister Michael could have been reading Elsie's palm. My aunt's quick feet carried her straight to Pain, which hounded her to the grave. Still a young woman, she was murdered by her white boyfriend in Rapid City, South Dakota. The local police didn't investigate because he was a prominent citizen and she was Indian. The reservation priest wouldn't bury her in the church yard because of the wild life she'd led. So she was buried just outside the fence. I wonder if I would hear her ticking heart in the unconsecrated ground?

If there is any justice, Aunt Elsie is tap-dancing in the afterlife as she used to as a child. She was always Ginger Rogers and my mother was Ruby Keeler. She is chatting it up with her hero, Joe Louis, who is giving her boxing tips. She is sitting on her father's lap and they are reading glossy magazines together. She is designing her own angel's wings by plucking ripe feathers off unsuspecting saints. She is telling God off-color jokes, one after the other, until He coughs and wheezes.

If there is any justice, Sister Michael is Pain's companion, and she is discovering that He is never satisfied. She is so tired and so depressed. She would like to walk away from Him, but every time she tries, He snatches her back with a hot paw.

My grandfather is hiding in a hole. His daughters pass food to him under the table. He has run out of cigarettes and reads each magazine ten times from cover to cover.

He calls his favorite daughters. "Will you find me some cigarettes?" he asks them. He is talking to their bare feet. Before they leave he gives them a nickel he's been saving. "Enough for two ice creams," he says, reaching up to place it in Elsie's hand.

My mother notices that his extended hand is shaking, and the other is massaging his sore stump. She starts to cry.

"Don't be such a sap," Elsie hisses in her ear, dragging my mother into the sun. "You've got to be tough!"

On the way to town Elsie and my mother see Old Man Standing Soldier asleep on the bench in front of his cabin.

"Beau-ti-ful Dreeeamer," they croon together, watching him with quick, crow eyes. "Beau-ti-ful Dreeeamer, wake unto MEE-E-E-E!"

Old Man Standing Soldier falls off the bench. "Get away from here!" he yells. "Líla síča, líla síča," *very bad*, he scolds.

My mother laughs so hard she almost pees in her pants.

The sisters come across Mary Halsey in her white anklets and black patent leather shoes. Her parents work for the Bureau of Indian Affairs so they always have money, even in hard times. They make Mary take off her shoes and socks so they can try them on.

"You'll stretch them out. You'll get them dirty!" she cries.

"Don't be so stingy," Elsie says, pulling up the loose legs of her overalls to look at the pretty shoes on her feet. My mother thinks the shoes are too tight when it is her turn. "Here," she hands them back to the weeping Mary.

Elsie and my mother are looking for cigarette butts in the street. They place the treasured tobacco in their pockets and wipe their hands on their thighs, careful in their work, serious. They are only children, unable to tell me why it is so important for them to put together a whole pack of cigarettes; beautiful, even, sweet-smelling. But I can see into their hearts. This is an offering to their buried father. They want him to close his eyes with pleasure as he smokes their cigarettes, blowing smoke rings that rise from the dirt floor to the ceiling.

# Always Running

Luis J. Rodríguez

LUIS J. RODRÍGUEZ was born in 1954 in El Paso, Texas, the son of Mexican immigrants. He grew up in Watts and East Los Angeles, and began writing in his teens. His autobiography, *Always Running, La Vida Loca: Gang Days in L.A.*, tells of his struggles with poverty, prejudice, drugs, and gang life. Now he is an award-winning poet and a writer, and is working with peacemakers among gang members in Los Angeles and other cities. Luis J. Rodríguez also runs Tia Chucha Press. He lives in Chicago with his family.

*Cry, child, for those without tears have a grief which never ends.*

—MEXICAN SAYING

This memory begins with flight. A 1950s bondo-spackled Dodge surged through a driving rain, veering around the potholes and upturned tracks of the abandoned Red Line trains on Alameda. Mama was in the front seat. My father was at the wheel. My brother Rano and I sat on one end of the back seat; my sisters Pata and Cuca on the other. There was a space between the boys and girls to keep us apart.

"*Amá, mira a Rano*," a voice said for the tenth time from the back of the car. "He's hitting me again."

We fought all the time. My brother, especially, had it in for La Pata—thinking of Frankenstein, he called her "Anastein." Her real name was Ana, but most of the time we went by the animal names Dad gave us at birth. I am Grillo, which means cricket. Rano stands for *rana*, the frog. La Pata is the duck and Cuca is short for *cucaracha:* cockroach.

The car seats came apart in strands. I looked out at the passing cars which seemed like ghosts with headlights rushing past the streaks of water on the glass. I was nine years old. As the rain fell, my mother cursed in Spanish intermixed with pleas to saints and "*la Santísima Madre de Dios.*" She argued with my father. Dad didn't curse or raise his voice. He just stated the way things were.

"I'll never go back to Mexico," he said. "I'd rather starve here. You want to stay with me, it has to be in Los Angeles. Otherwise, go."

This incited my mother to greater fits.

We were on the way to the Union train station in downtown L.A. We had our few belongings stuffed into the trunk and underneath our feet. I gently held on to one of the comic books Mama bought to keep us entertained. I had on my Sunday-best clothes with chewed gum stuck in a coat pocket. It could have been Easter, but it was a weeping November. I don't remember for sure why we were leaving. I just knew it was a special day. There was no fear or concern on my part. We were always moving. I looked at the newness of the comic book and felt some exhilaration of its feel in my hand. Mama had never bought us comic books before. It had to be a special day.

For months we had been pushed from one house to another, just Mama and us children. Mom and Dad had split up prior to this. We stayed at the homes of women my mom called *comadres*, with streams of children of their own. Some nights we slept in a car or in the living rooms of people we didn't know. There were no shelters for homeless families. My mother tried to get us settled somewhere but all indications pointed to our going back to the land of her birth, to her red earth, her Mexico.

The family consisted of my father Alfonso, my mom María Estela, my older brother, José René, and my younger sisters, Ana Virginia and Gloria Estela. I recall my father with his wavy hair and clean-shaven face, his correct, upright and stubborn demeanor, in contrast to my mother who was heavy-set with Native features and thick straight hair, often laughing heartily, her eyes narrowed to slits, and sometimes crying from a deep tomblike place with a sound like swallowing mud.

As we got closer to the Union station, Los Angeles loomed low and large, a city of odd construction, a good place to get lost in. I, however, would learn to hide in imaginative worlds—in books; in TV shows, where I picked up much of my English; in solitary play with mangled army men and crumpled toy trucks. I was so withdrawn it must have looked scary.

When my parents married, Mama was twenty-seven; Dad almost forty. She had never known any other man. He already had four or five children from three or four other women. She was an emotionally charged border woman, full of fire, full of pain, full of giving love. He was a stoic, unfeeling, unmoved intellectual who did as he pleased as much as she did all she could to please him. This dichotomous couple, this sun and moon, this *curandera* and biologist, dreamer and realist, fire woman and water man, molded me; these two sides created a lifelong conflict in my breast.

By the time Dad had to leave Ciudad Juarez, my mother had borne three of his children, including myself, all in El Paso, on the American side (Gloria was born later in East L.A.'s General Hospital). This was done to help ease the transition from alien status to legal residency. There are stories of women who wait up to the ninth month and run across the border to have their babies, sometimes squatting and dropping them on the pavement as they hug the closest lamppost.

We ended up in Watts, a community primarily of black people except for *La Colonia*, often called The Quarter—the Mexican section and the oldest part of Watts.

Except for the housing projects, Watts was a ghetto where

country and city mixed. The homes were mostly single-family units, made of wood or stucco. Open windows and doors served as air conditioners, a slight relief from the summer desert air. Chicken coops graced many a back yard along with broken auto parts. Roosters crowed the morning to birth and an occasional goat peered from weather-worn picket fences along with the millions of dogs which seemed to populate the neighborhood.

Watts fed into one of the largest industrial concentrations in the country, pulling from an almost endless sea of cheap labor; they came from Texas, Louisiana, Mississippi, Oklahoma, Arkansas . . . from Chihuahua, Sonora, Sinaloa and Nayarit. If you moved there it was because the real estate concerns pushed you in this direction. For decades, L.A. was notorious for restrictive covenants—where some areas were off limits to "undesirables."

Despite the competition for jobs and housing, we found common ground there, among the rolling mills, bucket shops and foundries. All day long we heard the pounding of forges and the air-whistles that signaled the shift changes in the factories which practically lay in our backyards.

Our first exposure in America stays with me like a foul odor. It seemed a strange world, most of it spiteful to us, spitting and stepping on us, coughing us up, we immigrants, as if we were phlegm stuck in the collective throat of this country. My father was mostly out of work. When he did have a job it was in construction, in factories such as Sinclair Paints or Standard Brands Dog Food, or pushing doorbells selling insurance, Bibles or pots and pans. My mother found work cleaning homes or in the garment industry. She knew the corner markets were ripping her off but she could only speak with her hands and in a choppy English.

Once my mother gathered up the children and we walked to Will Rogers Park. There were people everywhere. Mama looked around for a place we could rest. She spotted an empty spot on a park bench. But as soon as she sat down an American woman, with three kids of her own, came by.

"Hey, get out of there—that's our seat."

My mother understood but didn't know how to answer back in English. So she tried in Spanish.

"Look, spic, you can't sit there!" the American woman yelled. "You don't belong here! Understand? This is not your country!"

Mama quietly got our things and walked away, but I knew frustration and anger bristled within her because she was unable to talk, and when she did, no one would listen.

We never stopped crossing borders. The *Río Grande* (or *Río Bravo*, which is what the Mexicans call it, giving the name a power "Río Grande" just doesn't have) was only the first of countless barriers set in our path.

We kept jumping hurdles, kept breaking from the constraints, kept evading the border guards of every new trek. It was a metaphor to fill our lives—that river, that first crossing, the mother of all crossings. The L.A. River, for example, became a new barrier, keeping the Mexicans in their neighborhoods over on the vast east side of the city for years, except for forays downtown. Schools provided other restrictions: Don't speak Spanish, don't be Mexican—you don't belong. Railroad tracks divided us from communities where white people lived, such as South Gate and Lynwood across from Watts. We were invisible people in a city which thrived on glitter, big screens and big names, but this glamour contained none of our names, none of our faces.

The refrain "this is not your country" echoed for a lifetime.

Although we moved around the Watts area, the house on 105th Street near McKinley Avenue held my earliest memories, my earliest fears and questions. It was a small matchbox of a place. Next to it stood a tiny garage with holes through the walls and an unpainted barnlike quality. The weather battered it into a leaning shed. The back yard was a jungle. Vegetation appeared to grow down from the sky. There were banana trees, huge "sperm" weeds (named that because they stank like semen when you cut them), foxtails and yellowed grass. An avocado tree grew in the middle of the yard and its roots covered every bit of ground, tearing up cement walks while its branches scraped the bedroom windows. A sway of clothes on some lines filled the little bit of grassy area just behind the house.

My brother and I played often in our jungle, even pretending to be Tarzan (Rano mastered the Tarzan yell from the movies). The problem, however, was I usually ended up being the monkey who got thrown off the trees. In fact, I remember my brother as the most dangerous person alive. He seemed to be wracked with a scream which never let out. His face was dark with meanness, what my mother called *maldad.* He also took delight in seeing me writhe in pain, cry or cower, vulnerable to his own inflated sense of power. This hunger for cruelty included his ability to take my mom's most wicked whippings—without crying or wincing. He'd just sit there and stare at a wall, forcing Mama to resort to other implements of pain—but Rano would not show any emotion.

Yet in the streets, neighborhood kids often chased Rano from play or jumped him. Many times he came home mangled, his face swollen. Once somebody threw a rock at him which cut a gash across his forehead, leaving a scar Rano has to this day.

Another time a neighbor's kid smashed a metal bucket over Rano's head, slicing the skin over his skull and creating a horrifying scene with blood everywhere. My mother in her broken English could remedy few of the injustices, but she tried. When this one happened, she ran next door to confront that kid's mother.

The woman had been sitting on her porch and saw everything.

"*¿Qué pasó aquí?*" Mama asked.

"I don't know what you want," the woman said. "All I know is your boy picked up that bucket and hit himself over the head—that's all I know."

In school, they placed Rano in classes with retarded children because he didn't speak much English. They even held him back a year in the second grade.

For all this, Rano took his rage out on me. I recall hiding from him when he came around looking for a playmate. My mother actually forced me out of closets with a belt in her hand and made me play with him.

One day we were playing on the rooftop of our house.

"Grillo, come over here," he said from the roof's edge. "Man, look at this on the ground."

I should have known better, but I leaned over to see. Rano then pushed me and I struck the ground on my back with a loud thump and lost my breath, laying deathly still in suffocating agony, until I slowly gained it back.

Another time he made me the Indian to his cowboy, tossed a rope around my neck and pulled me around the yard. He stopped barely before it choked the life out of me. I had rope burns around my neck for a week.

His abuse even prompted neighborhood kids to get in on it. One older boy used to see how Rano tore into me. One day he peered over the fence separating his yard from ours.

"Hey, little dude . . . yeah, you. Come over here a minute," he said. "I got something to show you."

This time I approached with caution. Little good that did me: I stepped into a loop of rope on the ground. He pulled on it and dragged me through the weeds and foxtails, up the splintery fence, and tied it down on his side. I hung upside down, kicking and yelling for what seemed like hours until somebody came and cut me down.

The house on 105th Street stayed cold. We couldn't always pay the gas or light bills. When we couldn't, we used candles. We cleaned up the dishes and the table where we ate without any light, whispering because that's what people do in the dark.

We took baths in cold water, and I remember wanting to run out of the bathroom as my mother murmured a shiver of words to comfort me:

"*Así es, así será,*" she explained as she dunked me into the frigid bath.

One night, my parents decided to take us to a restaurant

since we had no heat to cook anything with. We drove around for a while. On Avalon Boulevard we found one of those all-night, ham-eggs-and-coffee places. As we pulled up, I curled up in the seat.

"No, I don't want to go in," I yelled.

"And why not?" my mother demanded. "*Por el amor de Dios*, aren't you hungry?"

I pointed a finger to a sign on the door. It read: "Come In. Cold Inside."

Christmases came with barely a whimper. Once my parents bought a fake aluminum tree, placed some presents beneath it, and woke us up early to open them up. Most of the wrappings, though, had been haphazardly put together because Rano had sneaked into the living room in the middle of the night and torn them open to take a peek. The presents came from a church group which gave out gifts for the poor. It was our first Christmas. That day, I broke the plastic submarine, toy gun and metal car I received. I don't know why. I suppose in my mind it didn't seem right to have things that were in working order, unspent.

My mother worked on and off, primarily as a *costurera* or cleaning homes or taking care of other people's children. We sometimes went with her to the houses she cleaned. They were nice, American, white-people homes. I remember one had a swimming pool and a fireplace and a thing called rugs. As Mama swept and scrubbed and vacuumed, we played in the corner, my sisters and I, afraid to touch anything. The odor of these houses was different, full of fragrances, sweet and nauseating. On 105th Street the smells were of fried lard, of beans and car fumes, of factory smoke and homemade brew out of backyard stills. There were chicken smells and goat smells in grassless yards filled with engine parts and wire and wood planks, cracked and sprinkled with rusty nails. These were the familiar aromas: the funky earth, animal and mechanical smells which were absent from the homes my mother cleaned.

Mama always seemed to be sick. For one thing, she was

overweight and suffered from a form of diabetes. She had thyroid problems, bad nerves and high blood pressure. She was still young then in Watts, in her thirties, but she had all these ailments. She didn't even have teeth; they rotted away many years before. This made her look much older until later when she finally obtained false ones. Despite this she worked all the time, chased after my brother with a belt or a board, and held up the family when almost everything else came apart.

One day, my mother asked Rano and me to go to the grocery store. We decided to go across the railroad tracks into South Gate. In those days, South Gate was an Anglo neighborhood, filled with the families of workers from the auto plant and other nearby industry. Like Lynwood or Huntington Park, it was forbidden territory for the people of Watts.

My brother insisted we go. I don't know what possessed him, but then I never did. It was useless to argue; he'd force me anyway. He was nine then, I was six. So without ceremony, we started over the tracks, climbing over discarded market carts and torn-up sofas, across Alameda Street, into South Gate: all-white, all-American.

We entered the first small corner grocery store we found. Everything was cool at first. We bought some bread, milk, soup cans and candy. We each walked out with a bag filled with food. We barely got a few feet, though, when five teenagers on bikes approached. We tried not to pay attention and proceeded to our side of the tracks. But the youths pulled up in front of us. While two of them stood nearby on their bikes, three of them jumped off theirs and walked over to us.

"What do we got here?" one of the boys said. "Spics to order—maybe with some beans?"

He pushed me to the ground; the groceries splattered onto the asphalt. I felt melted gum and chips of broken beer bottle on my lips and cheek. Then somebody picked me up and held me while the others seized my brother, tossed his groceries out, and pounded on him. They punched him in the face, in the stomach, then his face again, cutting his lip, causing him to vomit.

I remember the shrill, maddening laughter of one of the kids on a bike, this laughing like a raven's wail, a harsh wind's shriek, a laugh that I would hear in countless beatings thereafter. I watched the others take turns on my brother, this terror of a brother, and he doubled over, had blood and spew on his shirt, and tears down his face. I wanted to do something, but they held me and I just looked on, as every strike against Rano opened me up inside.

They finally let my brother go and he slid to the ground, like a rotten banana squeezed out of its peeling. They threw us back over the tracks. In the sunset I could see the Watts Towers, shimmers of seventy thousand pieces of broken bottles, sea shells, ceramic and metal on spiraling points puncturing the heavens, which reflected back the rays of a falling sun. My brother and I then picked ourselves up, saw the teenagers take off, still laughing, still talking about those stupid greasers who dared to cross over to South Gate.

Up until then my brother had never shown any emotion to me other than disdain. He had never asked me anything, unless it was a demand, an expectation, an obligation to be his throwaway boy-doll. But for this once he looked at me, tears welled in his eyes, blood streamed from several cuts—lips and cheeks swollen.

"Swear—you got to swear—you'll never tell anybody how I cried," he said.

I suppose I did promise. It was his one last thing to hang onto, his rep as someone who could take a belt whipping, who could take a beating in the neighborhood and still go back risking more—it was this pathetic plea from the pavement I remember. I must have promised.

It was a warm September day when my mother pulled me out of bed, handed me a pair of pants and a shirt, a piece of burnt toast, and dragged me by the arm toward 109th Street School. We approached a huge, dusty brick building with the school's name carved in ancient English lettering across the entrance. Mama hauled me up a row of steps and through two large doors.

First day of school.

I was six years old, never having gone to kindergarten because Mama wanted me to wait until La Pata became old enough to enter school. Mama filled out some papers. A school monitor directed us to a classroom where Mama dropped me off and left to join some parents who gathered in the main hall.

The first day of school said a lot about my scholastic life to come. I was taken to a teacher who didn't know what to do with me. She complained about not having any room, about kids who didn't even speak the language. And how was she supposed to teach anything under these conditions! Although I didn't speak English, I understood a large part of what she was saying. I knew I wasn't wanted. She put me in an old creaky chair near the door. As soon as I could, I sneaked out to find my mother.

I found Rano's class with the mentally disabled children instead and decided to stay there for a while. Actually it was fun; they treated me like I was everyone's little brother. But the teacher finally told a student to take me to the main hall.

After some more paperwork, I was taken to another class. This time the teacher appeared nicer, but distracted. She got the word about my language problem.

"Okay, why don't you sit here in the back of the class," she said. "Play with some blocks until we figure out how to get you more involved."

It took her most of that year to figure this out. I just stayed in the back of the class, building blocks. It got so every morning I would put my lunch and coat away, and walk to my corner where I stayed the whole day long. It forced me to be more withdrawn. It got so bad, I didn't even tell anybody when I had to go the bathroom. I did it in my pants. Soon I stank back there in the corner and the rest of the kids screamed out a chorus of "P.U.!" resulting in my being sent to the office or back home.

In those days there was no way to integrate the non-English-speaking children. So they just made it a crime to speak anything but English. If a Spanish word sneaked out in the playground, kids were often sent to the office to get swatted or to get detention. Teachers complained that maybe the children were saying bad things about them. An assumption of guilt was enough to get one punished.

A day came when I finally built up the courage to tell the teacher I had to go to the bathroom. I didn't quite say all the words, but she got the message and promptly excused me so I didn't do it while I was trying to explain. I ran to the bathroom and peed and felt good about not having that wetness trickle down my pants leg. But suddenly several bells went on and off. I hesitantly stepped out of the bathroom and saw throngs of children leave their classes. I had no idea what was happening. I went to my classroom and it stood empty. I looked into other classrooms and found nothing. Nobody. I didn't know what to do. I really thought everyone had gone home. I didn't bother to look at the playground where the whole school had been assembled for the fire drill. I just went home. It got to be a regular thing there for a while, me coming home early until I learned the ins and outs of school life.

Not speaking well makes for such embarrassing moments. I hardly asked questions. I just didn't want to be misunderstood. Many Spanish-speaking kids mangled things up; they would say things like "where the beer and cantaloupe roam" instead of "where the deer and antelope roam."

That's the way it was with me. I mixed up all the words. Screwed up all the songs.

Eventually I did make friends. My brother often brought home a one-armed Mexican kid named Jaime. Sometimes we all hung out together. Jaime lost his arm when he was a toddler. Somehow he managed to get the arm stuck in the wringer of one of those old washing machines which pulled the clothes through two rollers. It tore his arm off at the socket. But later he made up for it with soccer feet and even won a couple of fights with his one good arm.

And then there was Earl. I didn't really know him until one day when we lined up following recess, he pulled the *trenzas* of a Mexican girl in our class named Gabriela. We all liked Gabriela. But she was also quiet, like me. So Earl pulled on her braids, the girl wailed, turned around and saw me standing there. Just then the teacher ran out of the classroom. Gabriela pointed in my direction. The one who never says anything. Because of this, I suffered through an hour's detention, fuming in my seat the whole time.

Later that evening, Earl came to my sister's house where we were visiting. Seni answered the door and looked askance at him.

"What do you want?"

"I want to know if the boy upstairs can play."

"I don't know, I don't think so."

"Tell him I got some marbles. If it's okay, I'd like him to play with me."

"I don't know, I don't think so."

I looked down from the attic window and saw the tall, thin boy in striped shirt and blue jeans. Under an arm was a coffee can. Inside the can, marbles rattled whenever Earl moved.

But going through Seni was becoming a chore. Earl looked past her to a large, round woman in a print dress: My mom. She looked at the boy and then yelled up the stairs in Spanish.

"Go and play, Grillo," she said. "You stay in the attic all the time. Go and play. Be like other boys. *¡Ya!*"

Earl waited patiently as the Rodríguez household quaked and quavered trying to get me downstairs and into the yard. Finally, I came down. Earl smiled broadly and offered me the can of marbles.

"This is for taking the rap today, man."

I looked hard at him, still a little peeved, then reached out for the can and held the best marble collection I had ever seen. I made a friend.

Desert winds swept past the TV antennas and peeling fences, welcome breezes on sweltering dry summer days when people came out to sit on their porches, or beneath a tree in dirt yards, or to fix cars in the street.

But on those days the perils came out too—you could see

it in the faces of street warriors, in the play of children, too innocent to know what lurked about, but often the first to fall during a gang war or family scuffle.

One Hundred Third Street was particularly hard. It was the main drag in Watts, where most of the businesses were located, and it was usually crowded with people, including dudes who took whatever small change one might have in their pocket.

On days like that Rano, Jaime, Earl and I ventured out to the "third," as 103rd Street was called, or by the factories and railroad tracks playing dirt war with other kids. Other times we played on the rooftop and told stories.

"Did you ever hear the one about the half-man?" Earl asked.

"The what?" Jaime replied. "What's a half-man?"

"Well, he's a dude who got cut in half at the railroad tracks over there by Dogtown."

"Yeah, go on."

"So now he haunts the streets, half of him one place, the other half in another place—and he eats kids."

"Man, that's sick," Rano said. "But I got one for you. It's about *el pie*."

"What the hell is that?"

"*Pie* means foot in Spanish . . . and that's all it is! One big foot, walking around."

Gusts of winds swirled around the avocado tree branches as the moonlight cast uncanny shadows near where we related our tales.

"And you heard about *La Llorona*, right?" Rano continued.

"Oh, yeah, sure . . ."

"She's an old Mexican lady—"

"You mean Mrs. Alvarez?"

We laughed.

"Nah, this lady once got all her children and cut them up into tiny pieces."

"And . . ."

"And then she went all over the neighborhood, sprinkling bits of their bodies everywhere."

"And then . . ."

"So then God saw what she did and cursed her to walk the world, looking for her children—weeping—for all eternity. That's why she's called *La Llorona,* the weeping woman. And you know what, she picks up other kids to make up for the ones she's killed."

The leaves rustled, giving out an eerie sound. All of us jumped up, including Rano. Before anyone could say goodnight, we stumbled over one another, trying to get out of there, climbed off the roof, and ran through bedsheets and dresses hanging on a line, dashing like mad as we made our way home.

We changed houses often because of evictions. My dad constantly tried to get better work; he tried so many things. Although he was trained as a teacher, graduated with a degree in biology and had published Spanish textbooks in Mexico, in Los Angeles everyone failed to recognize his credentials. In Los Angeles, he was often no more than a laborer.

One day a miracle happened. My dad obtained a substitute teaching job in the San Fernando Valley, at Taft High School in Woodland Hills, teaching Spanish to well-off white children.

My dad must have thought we had struck oil or something. He bought a house in Reseda. In those days, this made us the only Mexican family around. It was a big house. It had three bedrooms, which meant the boys could have their own room, the girls theirs and my parents could be alone. It had two baths, a large, grassy yard and an upstanding, stucco garage.

I went to a school on Shirley Avenue which actually had books. I remember being chased back home a lot by the Anglo kids. But we were so glad to be in Reseda, so glad to be away from South Central Los Angeles.

Even my brother enjoyed success in this new environment. He became the best fighter in the school, all that he went through in Watts finally amounting to something. The big white kids tried to pick on him, and he fought back, hammered their faces with quick hands, in street style, after which nobody wanted to mess with him. Soon the bullies stopped chasing me home when they found out I was José's brother.

My dad went nuts in Reseda. He bought new furniture, a new TV, and he had the gall to throw away the old black-and-white box we had in Watts. He bought a new car. He was like a starving man in a candy store, partaking of everything, touching whatever he couldn't eat. He sat on a mountain of debt. But his attitude was "who cares?" We were Americans now. We were on our way to having a little bit of that dream. He was even doing it as a teacher, what he was trained for. Oh what a time it was for my father!

My mother, I could tell, was uncomfortable with the whole set-up. She shied away from the neighbors. The other mothers around here were good-looking, fit and well-built. My pudgy mom looked dark, Indian and foreign, no matter what money could buy. Except she got her false teeth. It seemed Mama was just there to pick up the pieces when my father's house of cards fell. She knew it would.

When it happened, it happened fast, decisively. It turned out Taft High School hired my father to teach Spanish on a temporary basis. Apparently the white kids couldn't understand him because of his accent. He wrote letters to the school board proposing new methods of teaching Spanish to American children so he could keep working. They turned them down, and Taft High School let him go.

We weren't in Reseda very long, less than a school year. Then the furniture store trucks pulled into the driveway to take back the new sofas, the washing machine, the refrigerator—even the TV. A "For Sale" sign jabbed into the front lawn. The new car had been repossessed. We pulled out of Reseda in an old beat-up Dodge. Sad faces on our neighbors were our farewell. I supposed they realized we weren't so bad for being Mexican. We were going back to an old friend—*pobreza.*

We moved in with Seni, her husband, and their two daughters. They were then occupying an apartment just outside East Los Angeles. Seni's girls were about the same age as me, my brother and sisters, although we were their uncles and aunts. They also had nicknames. Ana Seni was called Pimpos, which doesn't mean anything I know of. But Rano called her Beanhead and that took. Aidé was called La Banana because as a baby she had shades of blonde hair. They later had another daughter named Beca, also *güerita.*

Like most Latinos, we had a mixture of blood. My half-brother Alberto looked Caribbean. His mother came from Veracruz on the Caribbean side of Mexico which has the touch of Africa. The rest of us had different shades of Spanish white to Indian brown.

Uprooted again, we stuffed our things in a garage. The adults occupied the only two bedrooms. The children slept on makeshift bedding in the living room. My grandmother Catita also stayed with us. There were eleven of us crushed into that place. I remember the constant fighting. My dad was dumped on for not finding work. Seni accused her husband of having affairs with other women. Mama often stood outside alone, crying, or in the garage next to all our things piled on top of each other.

Rano and I sought refuge in the street.

One night, we came home late after having stocked up on licorice and bubble gum. We walked past police cars and an ambulance. Colored lights whirled across the tense faces of neighbors who stood on patches of grass and driveway. I pushed through low voices and entered the house: blood was splattered on a far wall.

Moments before, Seni had been brushing Pimpos' hair when, who knows why, she pulled at the long sections. The girl's screams brought in my sister's husband. An argument ensued. Vicious words. Accusations.

Seni then plucked a fingernail file from the bathroom sink. She flashed it in front of my brother-in-law's face. He grabbed for her hand. The nail file plunged into his arm. Mom and Dad rushed in, ramming my sister against the wall; nail file crashed steely bright onto the linoleum floor.

Soon after the incident, the landlord evicted us all. This was when my mother and father broke up. And so we began that car ride to the train station, on the way back to Mexico, leaving L.A., perhaps never to come back.

We pull into a parking lot at the Union station. It's like a point of no return. My father is still making his stand. Mama looks exhausted. We continue to sit in our seats, quiet now as Dad maneuvers into an empty space. Then we work our way out of the car, straightening our coats, gathering up boxes and taped-over paper bags: our "luggage." Up to this juncture, it's been like being in a storm—so much instability, of dreams achieved and then shattered, of a silence within the walls of my body, of being turned on, beaten, belittled and pushed aside; forgotten and unimportant. I have no position on the issue before us. To stay in L.A. To go. What does it matter? I've been a red-hot ball, bouncing around from here to there. Anyone can bounce me. Mama. Dad. Rano. Schools. Streets. I'm a ball. Whatever.

We are inside the vast cavern of the station. Pews of swirled wood are filled with people. We sit with our bags near us, and string tied from the bags to our wrists so nobody can take them without taking us too. My father turns to us, says a faint goodbye, then begins to walk away. No hugs. He doesn't even look at us.

"Poncho."

The name echoes through the waiting area.

"Poncho."

He turns. Stares at my mother. The wet of tears covers her face. Mama then says she can't go. She will stay with him. In L.A. I don't think she's happy about this. But what can a single mother of four children do in Mexico? A woman, sick all the time, with factory work for skills in a land where work is mainly with the soil. What good is it except to starve?

"*Está bien*," Dad says as he nears my mother. "We will make it, *mujer*. I know it. But we have to be patient. We have to believe."

Mama turns to us and announces we are not leaving. I'm just a ball. Bouncing outside. Bouncing inside. Whatever.

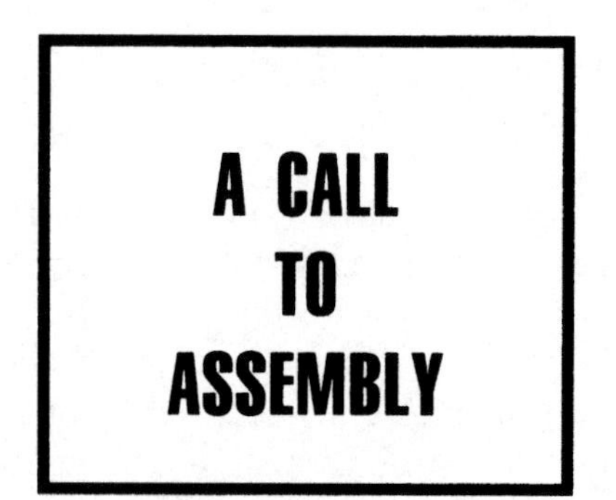

# A CALL TO ASSEMBLY

Willie Ruff

Acclaimed jazz musician and teacher WILLIE RUFF grew up in rural northwest Alabama. His early fascination with music and the many musical influences of his childhood are described in his autobiography *A Call to Assembly*, from which the following excerpt is taken. He has been a professor at Yale University for the past twenty years, has performed with Lionel Hampton, Miles Davis, and Duke Ellington, among others, and teamed with longtime friend Dwike Mitchell to form the Mitchell/Ruff Duo.

In the narrative that follows, Ruff's intense love of music and sound lead him in an unexpected direction.

In those preadolescent days, the delicious pleasures of my ear—the music and the stylish spoken language of our world—got out of hand and developed into serious distractions that caused me no end of problems at home. For a time, Mama Minnie insisted I was close to being retarded and a little "off." I was too much a listener. Impossible for me to concentrate on anything else if there was an ear diversion close by. I'd get stuck, for instance, at the barbershop for hours, listening to Doc Long and Wonderful C. Hill and Bitsy Pillar weaving the most colorful and engrossing stories. And when Tab and Ice-Truck Raymond came in, woofing with their boastful lying, I'd totally forget myself and linger for hours. Then suddenly I would realize I had a country skinning coming when I got back home, because Mama Minnie had ordered, "You get that head cut and get yourself back home and scrub that kitchen floor and sweep the front yard." It would be worse if I'd pass the railroad tracks and the hobo jungle on an errand and be pulled into it by the soulful strains of a traveling tramp's fiddle, or a mouth organ and a banjo, and forget the errand. Music and the spoken language of our world, which sounded like music, were taking over my life.

I was a slave to my ear and in love with my shackles.

But then I had a chance encounter with an altogether different kind of language, full of another kind of color, and it sucked me into its sphere and turned my impressionable ten-year-old mind completely upside down: it was sign language—talking with hands—the language of the deaf.

It happened when I went to work in a shoe repair shop, replacing a young black man who'd decided to go on to better things. This was a job that Mama Minnie was enthusiastic about, because it was an opportunity to learn a good trade while earning a little coin. The work was not hard to learn, and Mr. Steele, the owner, was a good teacher even though he could be touchy and sharp.

He started me off on the basics of nailing and gluing leather and rubber soles and heels, polishing and dyeing shoes, and making deliveries on the shop's nearly new Elgin bicycle—the absolute best part of the job for me. He kept me away from the big sewing machines, power cutters, and polishers, saying that when I got bigger he would teach me to use them safely. His wife worked the cash register. Mrs. Steele was a kind, quiet woman, whose presence in the shop took the edge off the old man's occasional abrasiveness. If, for instance, she went out to get him and herself a Coca-Cola, she'd bring me one, and she was polite enough to call me by my name and not "boy" all the time, as Mr. Steele did.

One day a man came into the shop and started rattling off talk on his hands with Mr. Steele. I was amazed that the boss could give it right back to this deaf fellow. Such expressive agility in his big shoemaker's dirty fingers made me wonder. He looked perfectly at home signing and even laughed out loud a couple of times with the deaf man before he left. Then I asked Mr. Steele, "Where did you learn to talk on your hands?"

"I was raised and taught my trade by my older brother," he said. "He was deaf, and he taught me shoemaking and the sign language. It ain't hard." After that, I kind of regarded the boss as a man of some mysterious inner substance, for I'd never heard or seen a real conversation in a foreign language before. This shoemaker speaking that silent secret code was an intoxicatingly exotic curiosity: "a white man with a language mojo," I told myself.

A few days later, Mr. Steele called me over to his workbench and said, "You remember that deaf man who was in here? Well, in a couple of weeks we're going to have company in the shop; a deaf boy is coming from the Talladega School for the Deaf and Blind to apprentice with me." He added a warning: "You got to learn how to talk to him. It'll be for your own good. You have to be careful working around deaf people, because they can sometimes be dangerous." I was confused. "Why are they dangerous?" I asked. Mr. Steele said, "Well, it's aggravating for them if they can't make you understand them or if they can't understand you. Then they're liable to hurt you. But I can teach you to talk on your hands in no time." That news provoked mixed feelings; I wanted desperately to learn to talk on my hands, but I wasn't looking forward to courting danger in the bargain.

We began my lessons that same day. In slack moments in the shop or during our rest breaks, he'd show me finger spelling. He'd been right about the ease of it; and it got to be fun saying the ABCs on my fingers. In a couple of days I could form all twenty-six letters without mistakes, and we began spelling out most of our conversation. Then, because I'd practiced at home and got pretty good showing off for Mama and the neighborhood, Mr. Steele said we'd not talk anymore at all, just spell. But I had trouble figuring out where one word ended and the next began, he spelled so quickly; I got better when he slowed down. Then he started teaching me real signs.

"Look here, boy," he said. "You can say a lotta things

with one or two motions of your hands. You can do it real quick and with practically no fuss." He held up one hand and, with the middle finger of the other hand, touched the first palm and then reversed the process, with motions that were quick as a snake. "Bet you can guess what that means, can't you?" No, I really couldn't. "Come on! Wake up, boy. Ain't you a Christian? That means Jesus Christ. Didn't you just see me point to the nails in Jesus' hands? Get it?" It was, I thought, a gruesome association to start me off with, but I had to admit it was interesting and efficient. Mr. Steele made me imitate the nails-in-the-hands sign until I got it down pat and with nearly the speed of a copperhead. Then I asked for more.

With his right hand, thumb extended, going up to touch his forehead, he said, "This means mother." Then, moving the same shape of the hand down so the thumb touched his chin, he said, "This means father." Then, back up with the same configuration, he thumbed his big nose and wiggled the other four fingers and said with an irreverent guffaw, "This means mother-in-law!" His wife cringed. Even Mr. Steele's cold crudeness and bad jokes couldn't dull my appetite for this powerful new magic. I was hooked.

When he told me that much of the sign language we use came from the American Indians, I felt proud of the Choctaw and Cherokee blood Mama said I had in me.

This, my very first foreign language, was starting to absorb me in its nonverbalness and its direct reference to thought and explicit meanings. I was falling in love with the magic of the live symbols shaped in the air between people doing all that communicating. Not suddenly, but gradually, I started to appreciate that these expressive hand shapes represented concepts that seemed bigger than just words to me, and I couldn't wait to learn as many as I could take in.

I went home one night after the lessons had progressed from the simple finger spelling to real signs and showed Mama some of what I was learning. I signed "love" for her, and she looked at my fists drawn in and folded across my chest and gave me an admiring smile. Then I showed her the thumb and forefinger of both hands opening both eyelids, and she hollered, "Wake up!" She said, "Why, baby, those are mind pictures you're making." She was just as proud as I'd been when I told her about the Indian origins of many signs. Every night when I brought her more new mind pictures, she'd guess at their meanings and marvel—at least she made me think it was marvelous—at my growing repertoire.

Then Smitty, the deaf boy from Talladega, joined us at the shoeshop. Smitty was about eighteen, a big, beefy blond with an appealing gentleness. It would have been hard not to like him. He was amused that I could even finger spell. That I also had learned quite a few signs from Mr. Steele really knocked him out. When I finger-spelled "Welcome," he shook my hand and with his opened right hand covered his mouth and moved the hand smartly away and down from his mouth, like a salute—the sign for "Thank you." I couldn't wait to get home that evening to lay that one on Mama. Smitty then signed for me to keep my face in his line of vision when addressing him and asked me not to pull on his clothes to get his attention unless it was an emergency, saying that was all I had to remember for us to get along just fine. Those were reasonable precautions, I thought, and with a combination of finger spelling and signing, I told him, "I hate people pulling on my clothes too." He lit up and shook with laughter, and my fears for all those dangers of the deaf Mr. Steele had warned me about flew right out the window.

By the time Smitty had been there a few weeks, I was getting better at signing and he and I were setting up routines to make our shopwork easier and more efficient. He told me about his school in Talladega and the trades—auto bodywork, piano tuning, shoe repair—it offered. He said one blind boy at the school was a wizard at auto body and fender work. He could feel the wrinkle in a fender with his hands and hammer it out with amazing precision.

I was soon overtaken by a sudden Helen Keller obsession. Until then, I'd not given Miss Keller's abilities at communicating as much thought as I had her prodigious book learning. Grown folk had said that when, as a little girl, she'd learned to read

Braille, she'd stayed with it so long and with such fierce tenacity that her fingers would bleed. Now I couldn't wait until "colored school day" rolled around at the Keller homeplace and museum in Tuscumbia. State law required the absolute racial separation of schoolchildren, and our school had to wait to visit the museum on a day when white children would not be there. I tried to picture in my mind what it would be like living in Miss Keller's dark and silent world. And when I asked myself, "What must it be like to never know music?" I shuddered at the horror of it. Now, for the first time, my Tuscumbia neighbor who'd moved on to world fame for her brilliance was coming into sharp focus in my imagination.

In an effort to better understand what it would be like to be Helen Keller, I clamped my eyes shut tight as if blind, and I stuffed cotton from one of Mr. Jim Clerk's cotton patches in my ears to make me close to deaf. I fumbled all over the house and in the yard. After practicing at home for a while, I left one day for work in that condition, trying—as Daddy Long used to say—to "rememberize" my route: the curbs, the traffic patterns, the trees that could bust your brains out if you were careless, and where the bad dogs were to be dodged along the way. Amazingly, I made it to work unscathed. Before long, with my eyes closed, I could negotiate downtown Sheffield pretty well. I was finding my way in my ersatz deaf-blind Helen Keller state until the day Ice-Truck Raymond sped across town with an overloaded truck and nearly ran me over as I crossed Second Street. He slammed on his brakes and hollered.

"Hey, fool, you think you was born with bumpers on your ass? You better open them damn eyes!" But I kept right on courting death as I practiced and explored Miss Keller's world, right up to the day when I got one of Mama Minnie's bad switch-whippings for not speaking back to Miss Callie, who'd spoken to me first and wondered why she'd had to. Mama Minnie wasn't ready to believe I'd not heard Miss Callie's greeting because I had cotton in my ears and missed seeing her because I was playing being blind. She'd preached my funeral after whipping me that day: "You are getting more foolish with every day the good Lord sends here, boy! You better throw away that dad-blamed cotton, mister, and use them good eyes God done give you if you don't want some more of my hickory!'' Mama Minnie with her quick and ready hickory was hard to reason with. I threw up my hands and promised to give up being Helen Keller on the streets of Sheffield.

One day at the shoeshop, I was in a conversation with Smitty and he was having trouble reading one of my signs. Though I thought I had it right, I obviously was faltering somewhere with a sign involving a complicated movement of the right fist. Mr. Steele, seeing my meaning and my problem right away, interrupted. ''Naw, boy!'' he said. ''Your problem is you got to hold that fist up like this.'' I held it up. ''No! Hold it like this: just like you gonna hit a nigger.''

I went cold. The color of deep red began crowding my vision, and an anger welled up in me that choked off my breath. I wanted to rage and strike out at him, but I was so stunned I just went weak. All I could think to do when I recovered a bit was to rip my apron off, make a fist with my right hand with the little finger up and move it toward my chest—the sign for ''I''—then, placing the first two fingers of my right hand in my left hand immediately snatching the two fingers out again. I'd signed: ''I quit!'' and was out the door.

I spent the next few days missing Smitty and the work. I couldn't have guessed that I'd miss sign language as much as I did. Most painful of all was my loss of respect for Mr. Steele. I couldn't bring myself to even mention having quit the job to Mama or Mama Minnie. I would just stay out of the house during regular work hours. I'd walk over to Tuscumbia and circle Helen Keller's homeplace and come back to tour Baptist Bottom. But then one day during the shop's regular lunch hour, Mama Minnie and my little sister and brother and I were in the front yard, when Mr. Steele's car pulled up. He called Mama Minnie out to the car and they talked for a while and he drove off. Mama Minnie came back and asked me what had happened at the shop to make me sass a grown person. I said I hadn't sassed anybody, I hadn't even said a word. "Don't you dast get smart with me, young-un! I know y'all talk on y'all's hands down there. Just tell me what did you say to the man when you quit that good job?"

"I quit because Mr. Steele said 'nigger,' " I said.

"Did he call you a nigger?"

"No, ma'am," I said, "but he used the word to me."

"*To* you?" she shot back, with strong emphasis on the "to." "Well, let me tell you something, child; this ol' world is hard. And as long as your hind parts point to the ground, you're gonna hear white folk use that word *and* a whole lot worse ones. Don't you know that?" I said I guess I did.

"Well, boy," she went on, "you can't get along in this here world if every time you hear somebody say 'nigger,' or something else you don't like, you gotta jump mad and swell up and quit your job and want to go to war. Willie Henry, let me tell you something. Sometimes you got to stoop to conquer, honey. I *know* what I'm talkin bout. Now, just as long as that white man in that shoeshop don't call *you* a nigger or hit you, it's foolish for you to quit—specially when you learning a good trade and making a little money." Mama Minnie completely missed the fact that I had no interest in the shoemaker's trade and that the dollar and a half a week I earned was nothing compared to the sign language I was learning.

"Well, suh," she said, "Mr. Steele said you're a good worker and a right apt learner. He'll take you back if you come on back after you eat. So you just cool off, and after you eat some of the dinner I got cooking on the stove, you go along on back to work and try to overlook whatever white folk say in front of you. As long as he ain't calling *you* names, pay it no mind." My spirit sank, but Mama was away at work, and my grandmother's word was law in the house until Mama came home. I was stuck.

Everybody knew Mama Minnie was one of the best cooks in Sheffield, but the meal she set before me that day tasted like gall. I felt like a condemned man swallowing his last meal, with all the taste drawn out of it.

When I stepped into the shoeshop, Smitty's face gleamed,

and he happily whapped the workbench with his hammer to signal Mr. Steele I was back. As I went for my work apron, hanging on the nail on the wall near Mr. Steele's last, I could see him gloating and silently asserting his supremacy over me. He was flushed with the victory he'd gained through Mama Minnie, and it was absolute. Suddenly my hand froze midair; it wouldn't move. I knew if I touched that apron something within me would die. My thoughts flashed back to that first sign he'd taught me—the gruesome "nails in the hands of Jesus"—and I knew my nailing days were done. A voice within me seemed to say, "There is nothing more for you in this place. Leave it. You're free!" I turned hard around and walked out of the shop toward Baptist Bottom and on to Tuscumbia, not caring what Mama Minnie was going to say or do to me when I got home.

I knew I'd lost my chance for learning more in my beloved sign language, but in the bargain I'd got in touch with a part of myself I'd not known before: the part I could always rely on to let me know just how far I was willing to stoop to conquer just to "get along" in Mama Minnie's hard ol' world.

# SOUND-SHADOWS OF THE NEW WORLD

## Ved Mehta

VED MEHTA was born in India. He came to the United States at the age of fifteen to pursue his education at the Arkansas School for the Blind in Little Rock, the subject of his autobiographical book, *Sound-Shadows of the New World,* from which the following excerpt is taken. He is the author of many other autobiographical books, including *Daddyji, Mamaji, Vedi,* and *The Ledge Between the Streams.* Ved Mehta is married and lives in New York City. In the narrative that follows, Ved Mehta has just arrived at Customs in New York.

At the airport, I was questioned by an immigration official. "You're blind—totally blind—and they gave you a visa? You say it's for your studies, but studies where?"

"At the Arkansas School for the Blind. It is in Little Rock, in Arkansas."

He shuffled through the pages of a book. Sleep was in my eyes. Drops of sweat were running down my back. My shirt and trousers felt dirty.

"Arkansas School is not on our list of approved schools for foreign students."

"I know," I said. "That is why the immigration officials in Delhi gave me only a visitor's visa. They said that when I got to the school I should tell the authorities to apply to be on your list of approved schools, so that I could get a student visa." I showed him a big manila envelope I was carrying; it contained my chest X-rays, medical reports, and fingerprint charts, which were necessary for a student visa, and which I'd had prepared in advance.

"Why didn't you apply to an approved school in the first place and come here on a proper student visa?" he asked, looking through the material.

My knowledge of English was limited. With difficulty, I explained to him that I had applied to some thirty schools but that, because I had been able to get little formal education in India, the Arkansas School was the only one that would accept me; that I had needed a letter of acceptance from an American school to get dollars sanctioned by the Reserve Bank of India; and that now that I was in America I was sure I could change schools if the Arkansas School was not suitable or did not get the necessary approval.

Muttering to himself, the immigration official looked up at me, down at his book, and up at me again. He finally announced, "I think you'll have to go to Washington and apply to get your visa changed to a student visa before you can go to any school."

I recalled things that Daddyji used to say as we were growing up: "In life, there is only fight or flight. You must always fight," and "America is God's own country. People there are the most hospitable and generous people in the world." I told myself I had nothing to worry about. Then I remembered that Daddyji had mentioned a Mr. and Mrs. Dickens in Washington—they were friends of friends of his—and told me that I could get in touch with them in case of emergency.

"I will do whatever is necessary," I now said to the immigration official. "I will go to Washington."

He hesitated, as if he were thinking something, and then stamped my passport and returned it to me. "We Mehtas carry our luck with us," Daddyji used to say. He is right, I thought.

The immigration official suddenly became helpful, as if he were a friend. "You shouldn't have any trouble with the immigration people in Washington," he said, and asked, "Is anybody meeting you here?"

"Mr. and Mrs. di Francesco," I said.

Mrs. di Francesco was a niece of Manmath Nath Chatterjee, whom Daddyji had known when he himself was a student, in London, in 1920. Daddyji had asked Mr. Chatterjee, who had a Scottish-American wife and was now settled in Yellow Springs, Ohio, if he could suggest anyone with whom I might stay in New York, so that I could get acclimatized to America before proceeding to the Arkansas School, which was not due to open until the eleventh of September. Mr. Chatterjee had written back that, as it happened, his wife's niece was married to John di Francesco, a singer who was totally blind, and that Mr. and Mrs. di Francesco lived in New York, and would be delighted to meet me at the airport and keep me as a paying guest at fifteen dollars a week.

"How greedy of them to ask for money!" I had cried when I learned of the arrangement. "People come and stay with us for months and we never ask for an anna."

Daddyji had said, "In the West, people do not, as a rule, stay with relatives and friends but put up in hotels, or in houses as paying guests. That is the custom there. Mr. and Mrs. di Francesco are probably a young, struggling couple who could do with a little extra money."

The immigration official now came from behind the counter, led me to an open area, and shouted, with increasing volume, "Fransisco! . . . Franchesca! . . . De Franco!" I wasn't sure what the correct pronunciation was, but his shouting sounded really disrespectful. I asked him to call for Mr. and Mrs. di Francesco softly. He bellowed, "Di Fransesco!"

No one came. My mouth went dry. Mr. and Mrs. di Francesco had sent me such a warm invitation. I couldn't imagine why they would have let me down or what I should do next.

Then I heard the footsteps of someone running toward us. "Here I am. You must be Ved. I'm Muriel de Francesco. I'm sorry John couldn't come." I noted that the name was pronounced the way it was spelled, and that hers was a Yankee voice—the kind I had heard when I first encountered Americans at home, during the war—but it had the sweetness of the voices of my sisters.

We shook hands; she had a nice firm grip. I had an impulse to call her Auntie Muriel—at home, an older person was always called by an honorific, like "Auntie" or "Uncle"—but I greeted her as Daddyji had told me that Westerners liked to be greeted: "Mrs. di Francesco, I'm delighted to make your acquaintance."

"You had a terrible trip, you poor boy. What a terrible way to arrive!" Mrs. de Francesco said in the taxi. "Imagine, everything stolen from a bag!"

One bag had contained clothes. The other, a holdall, had contained (in addition to some extra shirts) a number of ivory curios—statues of Lord Krishna, "no evil" monkeys, brooches with a little pattern on them—which Daddyji had bought with the idea that I could sell them at great profit. "You can take the ivory curios to a shop in Little Rock and ask the shop to sell them for you—on commission, of course," he had said. "In America, a lot of people earn and learn. Who knows? Maybe we could start an ivory-export-import business in a year or so, when I retire from government service." He was deputy director general of health services in the Indian government. "I expect there is a great deal of demand over there for hand-carved things." The fact that neither of us had ever sold even a secondhand gramophone didn't stop us from dreaming.

I didn't want Mrs. di Francesco to feel bad, so I made light of the theft. "The other bag is still full," I said.

"The ivory things must have been really valuable," she said. She had helped me fill out the insurance-claim forms. "What a bad introduction to America!"

"But it could have happened in Delhi."

She regaled the taxi-driver with the story, as if she and I were long-standing friends. "And we had to wait at the airport for two whole hours, filling out insurance forms. And he only knew the prices in rubles."

"Rupees," I said.

"Is that right?" the taxi-driver said, from the front seat. "Well, it shouldn't have happened to you, son."

I leaned toward the half-open window and listened for the roar of street crowds, the cries of hawkers, the clatter of tonga wheels, the trot of tonga horses, the crackle of whips, the blasts of Klaxons, the trills of police whistles, the tinkling of bicycle bells—but all I heard was the steady hiss and rush of cars. "In America, you can really travel fast and get places," I said.

Mrs. di Francesco took both my hands in hers and broke into open, unrestrained laughter. I have never heard a woman laugh quite like that, I thought.

"What are you laughing at?" I asked.

"I'd just noticed that all this time you had your hand in your breast pocket. Are you afraid of having your wallet stolen, too?"

I was embarrassed. I hadn't realized what I had been doing.

The taxi-driver took a sharp turn.

"Where are we?" I asked.

"On Broadway," Mrs. di Francesco said.

"Is Broadway a wide road?" I asked.

She laughed. "A very wide avenue—it's the center of the universe."

At home, the center was a circle, but here the center, it seemed, was a straight line. At home, I often felt I was on a merry-go-round, circling activities that I couldn't join in. Here I would travel in taxis amid new friends and have adventures. I tried to voice my thoughts.

"Poor boy, you have difficulty with the language," Mrs. di Francesco said, gently pressing my hand.

"English is difficult," I said, and I tried to make a joke. "When I was small and first learning English, I was always confusing 'chicken' and 'kitchen.' "

" 'Chicken' and 'kitchen,' " Mrs. di Francesco repeated, and laughed.

"I have enough trouble speaking English," the taxi-driver said. "I could never learn to speak Hindu."

"Hindi," I said, correcting him.

"You see?" the taxi-driver said.

Mrs. di Francesco laughed, and the taxi-driver joined in.

After a while, the taxi came to a stop. "Here we are at home, on a Hundred and Thirteenth Street between Broadway and Amsterdam," Mrs. di Francesco said.

Though I was carrying a bank draft for eighty dollars, I had only two dollars in cash, which a family friend had given me for good luck. I handed it to Mrs. di Francesco for the taxi.

"That won't be enough," she said.

"But it is *seven rupees!*" I cried. "At home, one could hire a tonga for a whole day for that."

"This is New York," she said. She clicked open her purse and gave some money to the taxi-driver.

The taxi-driver put my bags on the curb, shook my hand, and said, "If I go to India, I will remember not to become a tonga driver." He drove away.

We picked up the luggage. Mrs. di Francesco tucked my free hand under her bare arm with a quick motion and started walking. A woman at home would probably have cringed at the touch of a stranger's hand under her arm, I thought, but thinking this did not stop me from making a mental note that the muscle of her arm was well developed.

We went into a house, and walked up to Mr. and Mrs. di Francesco's apartment, on the fourth floor. Mr. di Francesco opened the door and kissed Mrs. di Francesco loudly. Had a bomb exploded, I could not have been more surprised. They'll catch something, I thought. I had never heard any grownups kissing at home—not even in films.

Mr. di Francesco shook my hand. He had a powerful grip and a powerful voice. He took me by the shoulder and almost propelled me to a couch. "This is going to be your bed," he said. "I'm sorry I couldn't come to the airport. Anyway, I knew you wouldn't mind being greeted by a charming lady." He doesn't have a trace of the timid, servile manner of music masters and blind people at home, I thought.

"We had a delightful ride from the airport," I said.

Mr. di Francesco wanted to know why we were so late, and Mrs. di Francesco told him about the theft.

"What bad luck!" he said.

"But I got here," I said.

"That's the spirit," he said, laughing.

"John, thank you for starting dinner," Mrs. di Francesco said from what I took to be the kitchen.

"Oh, you cook!" I exclaimed. I had never heard of a blind person who could cook.

"Yes, I help Muriel," he said. "We don't have servants here, as they do in your country. We have labor-saving devices." He then showed me around the apartment, casually tapping and explaining—or putting my hand on—various unfamiliar things: a stove that did not burn coal or give out smoke; an ice chest that stood on end and ran on electricity; a machine that toasted bread; a bed for two people; and a tub in which one could lie down. I was full of questions, and asked how natural gas from the ground was piped into individual apartments, and how people could have so much hot water that they could lie down in it. At home, a husband and wife never slept in one bed, but I didn't say anything about that, because I felt shy.

"Do you eat meat?" Mrs. di Francesco asked me from the kitchen. "Aunt Rita—Mrs. Chatterjee—didn't know."

"Yes, I do eat meat," I called back to her. I started worrying about how I would cut it.

Mrs. di Francesco sighed with relief. "John and I hoped that you weren't a vegetarian. We're having spaghetti and meatballs, which are made of beef. Is that all right?"

I shuddered. As a Hindu, I had never eaten beef, and the mere thought of it was revolting. But I recalled another of Daddyji's sayings, "When in Rome, do as the Romans do," and said, "I promised my father that I would eat anything and everything in America and gain some weight."

Mrs. di Francesco brought out the dinner and served it to us at a small table. "The peas are at twelve and the spaghetti and meatballs at six," she said. I must have looked puzzled, because she added, "John locates his food on a plate by the clock dial. I thought all blind people knew—"

"You forget that India has many primitive conditions,"

Mr. di Francesco interrupted. "Without a doubt, work for the blind there is very backward."

I bridled. "There is nothing primitive or backward in India."

There was a silence, in which I could hear Mr. di Francesco swallowing water. I felt very much alone. I wished I were back home.

"I didn't mean it that way," Mr. di Francesco said.

"I'm sorry," I said, and then, rallying a little, confessed that Braille watches were unheard of in India—that I had first read about them a year or so earlier in a British Braille magazine, and then it had taken me several months to get the foreign exchange and get a Braille pocket watch from Switzerland.

"Then how do blind people there know what time it is—whether it is day or night?" Mr. di Francesco asked.

"They have to ask someone, or learn to tell from the morning and night sounds. I suppose that things *are* a little backward there. That is why I had to leave my family and come here for education."

"The food is getting cold," Mrs. di Francesco said.

I picked up my fork and knife with trembling fingers and aimed for six. I suddenly wanted to cry.

"You look homesick," Mrs. de Francesco said.

I nodded, and tried to eat. A sense of relief engulfed me: we had mutton meatballs at home all the time, and they didn't require a knife. But the relief was short-lived: I had never had spaghetti, and the strands were long and tended to bunch together. They stretched from my mouth to my plate—a sign of my Indian backwardness, I thought. I longed for the kedgeree at home, easily managed with a spoon.

Mrs. di Francesco reached over and showed me how to wrap the spaghetti around my fork, shake it, and pick it up. Even so, I took big bites when I thought that Mrs. di Francesco was not looking—when she was talking to Mr. di Francesco. Later in the meal, it occurred to me that I was eating the food Daddyji had eaten when he was a student abroad. I resolutely bent my face over the plate and started eating in earnest.

Mrs. di Francesco took away our plates and served us something else, and I reached for my spoon.

"That's eaten with a fork," she said.

I attacked it with a fork. "It is a pudding with a crust!" I cried. "I have never eaten anything like it."

"It's not a pudding—it's apple pie," Mrs. de Francesco said. "By the way, we're having scrambled eggs for breakfast. Is that all right?"

I confessed that I didn't know what they were, and she described them to me.

"Oh, I know—rumble-tumble eggs!" I exclaimed. "I like them very much."

They both laughed. "British—Indian English is really much nicer than American English," Mr. di Francesco said. "You should keep it. In fact, I'll adopt 'rumble-tumble.' "

I felt sad that I had come to America for my studies instead of going to England first, as Daddyji had done. But no school in England had accepted me.

"We've heard so much about India from Uncle Manmath," Mrs. di Francesco said. "It must be a very exciting place."

"Yes, tell us about India," Mr. di Francesco said.

I felt confused. I couldn't think of what to say or how to say it.

"You look tired," Mrs. di Francesco said, patting me on the arm.

"I cannot think of the right English words sometimes," I said.

Mrs. di Francesco cleared some things off the table and said, "Don't worry. Now that you're here, your English will improve quickly."

She went to the kitchen and started washing the plates while Mr. di Francesco and I lingered at the table—much as we might at home.

I asked Mr. di Francesco how he had become self-supporting and independent, with a place of his own.

"You make it sound so romantic, but it's really very simple,'' he said. He spoke in a matter-of-fact way. ''I spent twelve years at the Perkins Institution for the Blind, in Massachusetts. I entered when I was seven, and left when I was nineteen.''

''Perkins!'' I cried. ''I have been trying to go there since I was seven. First, they would not have me because of the war. But after the war they would not have me, either—they said that I would end up a 'cultural misfit.' ''

''What does that mean?''

''They said that bringing Eastern people to the West at a young age leads to 'cultural maladjustment'—and they said, 'Blindness is a maladjustment in itself.' ''

''But now you're here. I'll call Perkins tomorrow and tell them that the damage is already done, and that your cultural maladjustment would be much worse if you were to end up in Arkansas.'' He laughed.

''Do you really think they will take me? Dr. Farrell, the director at Perkins, is a very stubborn man.''

''They certainly should. Unlike Massachusetts, Arkansas is a very poor state. Arkansas School for the Blind is a state school. They are required to accept all the blind children in the state free of charge. In fact, you'll probably be the only one there paying for board and tuition. The school is bound to have a lot of riff-raff. It's no place to improve your English. In Arkansas, you'll lose all your nice Britishisms and acquire a terrible Southern drawl. You have to go to Perkins. I know Dr. Farrell.''

I was excited. ''Perkins is said to be the best school for the blind anywhere. How did you like it? How was your life there?''

''Life at Perkins? It was probably no different from that of millions of other kids. We played and studied.'' He added obligingly, ''It was a lot of fun.''

Fun—so that's what it was, I thought. That is the difference between all the things he did at school and all the things I missed out on by not going to a good school.

''And after Perkins?''

''After Perkins, I studied voice at the New England Conservatory, where Muriel and I met. Then I came to New York, started giving voice lessons, married Muriel, and here I am.''

"There must be more to tell."

"There really isn't."

"Did Mrs. di Francesco's parents not object? She is sighted."

"I wasn't asking to marry Muriel's parents. She could do what she pleased. This is America."

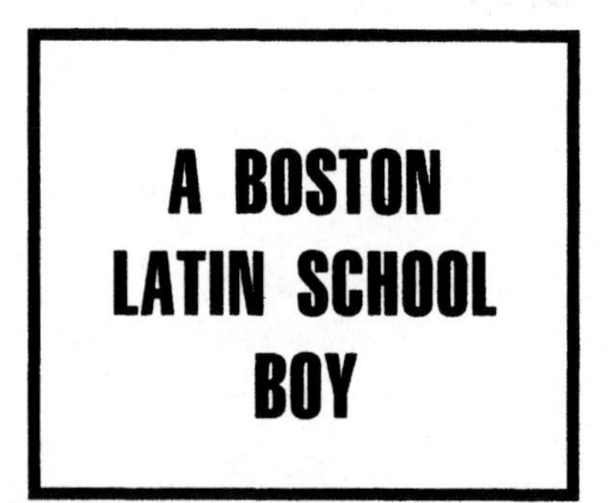

# A BOSTON LATIN SCHOOL BOY

Lee A. Daniels

LEE A. DANIELS was born in Chicago in 1948 and grew up in Boston. He graduated from Boston Latin School, the subject of this piece, and from Harvard University. He has worked as a television reporter for WGBH (Boston), a reporter and editorial writer for the *Washington Post*, and a reporter for the *New York Times*. Presently he teaches expository writing at Harvard College and is a fellow of the W. E. B. DuBois Institute for Afro-American Research of Harvard University.

When I was born in 1948, black Americans, no matter what their aspirations or abilities, were confined to a small corner of American life. The most likely consideration of my family's circumstances then would have confidently predicted that would be my fate as well.

The Daniels and Harris families, my forebears, were working-class people, people of the soil, people who lived in the shadow of history. My mother, Virginia Naomi Harris, had grown up in Boston and graduated from high school. My father, Lloyd Abbott Daniels, born in Oklahoma Territory, had been able to go to school to the eleventh grade only because his father had continually shipped him out to various relatives in cities in the West and Midwest.

We could not trace our family line back beyond three generations, and those generations were, for me, peopled by shadowy figures: my mother's grandmother, born in slavery and dead by my fourth year; my father's father, who married four times and sired eight children, none of whom, other than my father, my siblings and I have ever met; my mother's father, who lived in Washington, D.C., where she was born, wore well-tailored clothes, and was a man whom "nobody ever messed with." Of all my forebears, until I was an adult, I knew only my mother's mother, Mary Harris Raynor.

As scanty as this family history was, most of it I learned only as an adult. During childhood and adolescence I sensed an unwillingness among my parents and grandmother to discuss the past in our presence except in the most general of terms. Was there a deliberate decision to keep the past from us? Why? Was there too much pain, humiliation, anger? Was the past too full of dreams thwarted by racial prejudice, whose telling could stunt our own aspirations, to be talked about? Did they think it was better for us not to know how circumscribed life had been and was for Americans who were black?

I lived in Chicago until I was ten and was vaguely aware of the meaning of race and racism. But I had an idyllic childhood, meandering through grade school, having crushes on my second- and third-grade teachers, and becoming a rabid baseball and football fan. We had no television until I was eight, but we did have the twenty-volume set of the 1947 *World Book Encyclopedia* my parents had bought that year after my brother, Lloyd Jr., was born. That purchase is the reason why my knowledge of both fairy tales and comics would forever remain scanty: it was the encyclopedia I read, again and again and again, throughout my childhood.

My father's earnings, as a factory worker and later as a longshoreman, a job he held until his death in 1993, must have been meager. But my parents had their own family-planning strategy—my sisters, Leslie and Lois, were born within two years of each other, and then, twelve years later, Lloyd and I were born within two years of each other—which helped ease the financial strain of having four children. The girls were in college or married by the time we boys entered kindergarten. I didn't understand we were poor until I was a teenager. We were well-fed and well-clothed due to Mom's scrupulous attention to food sales and constant trips to rummage sales, and we were subjected to a cultural enrichment program which, I later realized, indicated my parents' ambitions for us.

There was church every Sunday at Greater Walters AME Zion Church. There were the Cub Scouts and the Boy Scouts, and the barely tolerated piano lessons (Mom was a very good pianist). There were the trips to the Lincoln Park and Grant Park zoos, the Chicago Museum of Art, and my favorite, the Field Museum of Natural History and the Museum of Science and Industry. And there were the piles of magazines and newspapers, from *Ebony* to *National Geographic* to *Reader's Digest* to the Chicago papers and the Sunday *New York Times*, that lay in bookcases, on tables, and on the floor throughout the living room. I read anything I could get my hands on.

All this encouragement to achieve, and hope mixed with expectation that we would, was implicit. From childhood through high school, my parents never said anything to us about going to college, or even about doing well in school; no heart-to-heart talks about the importance of education, no discussions of what we were reading or doing in school. In fact, they would periodically advise us to learn a trade so that we'd be able to support ourselves as adults. This got to be tiresome because neither Lloyd nor I ever doubted that it was a pose: we *knew* we were expected to do well in school and go on to college.

Despite the cultural regimen and my subconscious sense of their expectations, however, all through grade school I was an erratic student whose interest in the schoolwork depended on whether the teacher captured my interest.

That continued when we moved to Boston in 1958. Actually, it was a move back to Boston for everyone else but me, because Boston was our "family seat," the place where Mom had grown up, where Mom and Dad had met and married, where my two sisters and brother were born, and where my grandmother, whom we called Booba, lived for more than fifty years.

I had visited Boston twice before then. But the only Boston I really knew was the one described in our *World Book Encyclopedia*—the Cradle of Liberty, the Athens of America, the Hub of the Nation. There was nothing in the encyclopedia about Boston's black ghetto.

In 1958 Boston's miniscule black population—just nine percent of its nearly seven hundred thousand citizens—was largely confined to an L-shaped area southwest of downtown that encompassed two neighborhoods, the South End and Roxbury. Perched on a gently rising hill, Roxbury was home to most of Boston's blacks, including most of its tiny black middle class who lived in a small area of well-maintained homes and apartment buildings called Sugar Hill. Actually, like any ghetto, Roxbury had a significant number of dilapidated buildings, but Sugar Hill's ambiance of respectability and relative well-being lent the whole area an unmistakable cachet.

The South End, bordered by Roxbury, the tony Back Bay, and downtown, was the flats, Boston's traditional port-of-entry for Chinese, southern and eastern European immigrants, and black migrants from the South. It was a polyglot neighborhood whose core was solidly black. At the center of that core was "the Strip," the intersection of Massachusetts and Columbus avenues, one of the city's two black red-light districts. My grandmother's apartment was at 615 Columbus Avenue, a block and a half from the intersection. I lived there from 1958 until the spring of my senior year in high school.

Life in the South End pricked the idyllic bubble of my childhood. For me life on Chicago's South Side had been trips to the museum, and baseball and football games with neighborhood pals. I had read the *Reader's Digest* and saw an image of life that I didn't consider very much different from my own. I had read the encyclopedia's biographies of the presidents and had idly dreamed that one day I, too, would be president. I grew out of that in Boston. It being staid Boston, the strip was relatively innocuous as such areas go, but I was older and could more clearly understand what was around me.

We lived just across the Boston & Maine Railroad tracks from Northeastern University, Symphony Hall, Horticultural Hall, the New England Conservatory of Music, the Mother Church of the Christian Science Church, the Boston Museum of Fine Arts, and other Back Bay institutions of high culture; all were within fifteen minutes' walking distance.

But now the phrase "across the tracks" took on real meaning for me. I could see there was a difference in the two neighborhoods—in the way the apartment buildings were maintained, in the way the police patrolled them, in the way the commuters driving through them looked at the buildings and the people on the street. I understood, without thinking about it, that the difference was one of race.

Mom enrolled us in the New England Conservatory of Music, five minutes' walk from our doorstep, to continue our piano lessons, but peer influence now seemed more powerful than that of my parents. After three years of practicing as little as possible, I gained her disappointed assent to drop the lessons. Lloyd followed a short time later.

I had got in with what passed in sedate Boston for a group of incipient juvenile delinquents and spent much of my time running the streets, looking at the older teenagers and the pimps and hustlers on the strip. Beyond the boundaries of my relatively small "roaming area" were the fighting, or "bopping," gangs with their wonderfully romantic names—the Marcaire Dukes, the Unknowns, the Elgents, the Band of Angels, the Lord Sophisticates. They were not quite role models for me, but I intently studied their ways of walking and posing, their style of dress, and their inventive use of profanity.

Despite my fascination with the underside of the ghetto, however, my parents's influence dominated my attitudes and actions far more than I would then have acknowledged. I never engaged in any criminal activity—with one exception: at twelve I joined the short-lived fad that gripped our peer group of breaking into parking meters for the bountiful and easily disposable supply of dimes they yielded.

But that descent into crime stopped when two policemen spotted Lloyd and me breaking open a meter on Massachusetts Avenue near the Christian Science Church. We easily outran their half-hearted pursuit—but not before Lloyd grabbed me and virtually hurled me in another direction as I was about to run into a cul-de-sac. The vision I had that night of being caught, booked, and fingerprinted, and then having to face Mom and Dad, was enough to extinguish for good whatever delinquent inclinations I may have harbored.

I was never religious, but the black church remained a central part of my life until college because of its importance in black communities. I drank no liquor until I was seventeen, and then only sparingly at parties. I smoked only at parties, it being the "social" thing to do. And, despite several episodes of heavy petting, I remained celibate until sophomore year in college.

The reason for that, I knew even then, stemmed from the first and only talk Mom ever had with us about sex. When I was thirteen, she had called us to her one day, told us to sit down, and quietly said, "You're at the age where you're able to get a girl pregnant. I want you to know that if you do, you will drop out of school, marry her, and get a job to support her and the baby. Do you understand?" We nodded. She never said anything else about sex to us, probably because she knew she didn't have to.

School I found completely uninteresting. At the elementary level some of our textbooks were fifty years old and the lessons were equally outdated. I rarely had homework. Only later would I understand that these things represented the indifference, at best, toward us of the people who controlled the Boston school system. I spent my two years there eagerly awaiting recess, getting milk for the class at lunch, and cleaning the blackboards during the last minutes of the last period, two of the duties awarded to "nice" boys. Nonetheless, I gained honor grades often enough to qualify for entrance to the Boston Latin School, the city's top public secondary school, which began in the seventh grade and which Lloyd had entered the previous year.

(It wasn't that simple, however, I've come to realize. I know now neither Lloyd nor I would have gotten to Latin if Mom had not made it clear to our teachers that we were bright boys who were to be pushed ahead and pushed on to Latin—and if they had not agreed with her.)

Boston Latin was a unique institution in American education. Its bedrock was its demanding classical curriculum—four to five years of Latin instruction was required; its rigor—only a third of the students who entered graduated; and, in pedagogical matters, its obsessive resistance to innovation. Philip Marson, a former teacher, wrote in *Breeder of Democracy*, his book about the school, that Boston Latin considered almost everything about itself, "fixed, inflexible, and proven" by the achievements of its alumni.

And history did provide some justification for obstinacy. Latin had been founded in 1635, five years after Boston itself and a year before Harvard College, to which, until the early 1950s, it would send one third to half of its small graduating classes.

In colonial times and the early 1800s those classes were comprised of sons of Boston's Yankee elite—among them, Cotton Mather, John Hancock, Harrison Gray Otis, Wendell Phillips, Charles Sumner, Ralph Waldo Emerson, and Henry Ward Beecher (father of Harriet Beecher Stowe, the author of *Uncle Tom's Cabin*). It had schooled four signers of the Declaration of Independence, and scores of prominent merchants, ministers, educators, and politicians. Benjamin Franklin had been a student, but had left to make his fortune long before he would have graduated. Naturally, Latin counted him an alumnus anyway. Since the 1880s, however, when Boston's "Brahmins" fled the public schools to avoid the "immigrant invasion," Latin's classes consisted largely of bright middle-class and working-class boys from the white ethnic groups: George Santayana, Bernard Berenson, Roy E. Larsen, a co-founder of *Time* magazine, Theodore H. White, Robert Coles, Leonard Bernstein. And there were always a small number of black boys, too, such as Clifton R. Wharton, Jr., the educator, corporate executive, and diplomat.

(Latin was for boys only until the early 1970s. Its counterpart, Girls' Latin School, had been established in 1878 and had an equally distinguished history. Both are now co-educational. Girls' Latin changed its name to Boston Latin Academy.)

Lloyd had entered Latin the previous year and was already showing the diligence that would mark his smooth passage through it. But I was different. I was contemptuous of it. Perhaps my attitude sprang from a desire to distinguish myself from a good-student brother I had always followed through school. It was certainly influenced by my street-corner friends, who sneered at Latin as a school for "smart boys." (Latin's book covers, with which textbooks had to be covered, carried the school's seal—the statue of the mythological twins, Romulus and Remus, being suckled by the she-wolf that raised them. This was not a book cover that would appeal to most boys in any neighborhood, and I did not openly carry my books outside of school until I was a freshman.) But Mom insisted, and in September 1960, off to Latin I went.

I wasn't at all concerned with staying there. As a result, my grades fluctuated wildly, and one June morning my homeroom teacher sadly told me I'd have to repeat the seventh grade.

Initially the news had little effect on me. But the more I thought about it on the way home that afternoon, the more uneasy I became. I realized I wasn't at all comfortable with being labelled dumb, inferior, a nobody. My mother, who must have long been aware of what was happening from the grades on my report cards, received the news without comment: a quick, impassive glance up from her sewing; a moment's pause; and then, turning again to her work, she quietly said that I could transfer to another school if I wished. I was stunned and suddenly deeply embarrassed. I hadn't expected the offer and, walking quickly from the room, refused it, saying, "No. I'll stay at Latin."

And I was immediately struck by my refusal of the offer I thought I had been waiting for. I would not fully understand why I had done so until years later—the realization probably would have been too devastating for me then: that I was deeply ashamed at having so obviously disappointed my mother. Her very impassiveness seemed to underscore my belief that she had given up on me, that she had come to the conclusion that I had turned out to be no good.

I would have been treading on dangerous ground psychologically to have acknowledged that to myself then, for the whole episode had brought closer to the surface of my mind the feelings of inferiority I had always held about myself. I didn't then perceive these feelings as related to race. It was a personal matter: I felt that I wasn't really worthy of being loved, that I was not good-looking, that I didn't have a personality that attracted people, that I was ordinary, ordinary, ordinary. And my failure at the Latin School seemed to confirm all those self-accusations.

Later I would understand that the feeling of having been publicly discredited had immediately unleashed the fierce need for achievement that was to propel me through the Latin School and Harvard. But then, alone in my room, I took another, less burdensome approach: I accepted the no-less-true fact that I actually liked the Latin School and wanted to stay.

Despite my dilatory attitude that year, I had been attracted by Latin's history: I was fascinated that the school I was attending was 325 years old, that it had existed when New England was still a wilderness to the European colonists and the birth of the United States of America was yet more than a century in the future, that scores of its alumni had played central roles in the life of Boston and of the nation. I would look at the pictures of previous Latin School classes, the old drawings from the school's century-old magazine, and cartoons and clippings of football games with our archrival high school, Boston English, that lined the halls, and daydream of what life had been like for these boys and how I was following in their footsteps.

That seemed literally true. The Latin School building then was less than fifty years old; but its neoclassical exterior and its interior, worn and seemingly indelibly begrimed by decades of hard use, made it feel much older.

More important was the fact that as an institution Latin had really changed very little since the mid-1800s: its absorbing pride was rooted in its exacting, classical curriculum. It was an institution where we students called our teachers "masters," where we stood to speak to them, where "approbation" and "approbation with distinction," the equivalent of honors and high honors, were the rewards for conquering the demands of the school year's eight marking periods, where misdemeanor marks, detention after school, and the dreaded "censure" governed our conduct, and where blazers—called "sack coats" in the Latin School lexicon—and ties were required in my upperclass years. Students who did not take to this regimen did not last there.

It was easy for someone like me, whose fascination with history stemmed in part from a subconscious need to find my own place in society, to believe that the outsized role Latin had once played in the nation's history was continuing—after all, the President's father, Joseph P. Kennedy, had graduated from Latin in 1908. Kennedy had been a stellar athlete and class leader as a Latin School student, and he embodied the promise that Latin held out to the poor and immigrant families of Boston: it was the gateway to success in life. That link had brought the Latin School Band an invitation to march in the Inaugural Parade and, I shared in Latin's immense pride.

At Latin School, my interest in history, reading, and in the encyclopedia, which had virtually disappeared since we had come to Boston, began to return. Having seen the surprise and reappraisal in adult and even youthful eyes when the magic words of where I went to school were spoken, I understood there were certain advantages to being a Latin School boy. My attendance there set me apart and marked me as special, and I discovered that having people—and myself—think I was special was what I wanted and needed.

My remaining at Latin began pushing me towards academic achievement. Joining the varsity track squad (students in all six of Latin's grades were eligible for varsity competition), I was introduced to the school's extracurricular life; the training and competition began to consume the afternoon hours, and homework accounted for the evening hours I had once spent in the streets. My track career was soon to be interrupted, but through track I came to know other teenagers in Roxbury who were also following a college-bound path. Gradually, my circle of friends expanded; we viewed going to college as a given.

Latin School was my direct link with history, my connection with a long line of achievers that stretched back beyond the country's founding. That all of these alumni were white—I didn't know any black Latin School alumni then—didn't matter. Nor did it matter what their accomplishments were, nor that some of them undoubtedly would have considered me "inferior." What did matter was that they had gone through the same school I was going through. I reasoned that I could not be less intelligent, less able to do the schoolwork than at least some of them; if all of these people could do the work at Latin, then I could, too.

The realization that I liked Latin School also made it possible for me to begin, slowly and largely without thinking about it, to appreciate Boston and assimilate its history and character.

Boston's history was palpable to me precisely because the city in the early 1960s was what it had been for decades: a place whose assembly of world-famous hospitals, colleges and universities, and institutions of high culture obscured the fact that it had largely made time stand still. The Boston of the early 1960s was a city whose last skyscraper, just twenty-six stories tall, had been built in 1952, a city whose transit system stopped operating at 1:00 A.M., a city whose "blue laws" required that most stores be closed on Sunday.

In reality, Boston was deliberately, fervently provincial. And yet the fact that it seemed connected with the modern world from a very long way off made it a wonderful place for me to grow up. Yes, it could be said that Boston looked so resolutely to the past in order to hide from the present and the future. But its provincialism also preserved traditions and values—stability, integrity, discretion, and the promotion of intellectual achievement and service to the community—that deeply attracted me. Boston was "different," "eccentric," "peculiar," which to me translated as independent-minded and defiantly proud of it. I felt comfortable and nourished.

For example, one reason I never felt poor as an adolescent

was because Boston's culture stressed moderation and frugality; affluence was not something that respectable Bostonians, of whatever color, displayed.

Another benefit to growing up in Boston was that, because of the city's small size and insular character, black Boston lacked the sharp social divisions that existed in other cities between those teenagers who aspired to college and those who did not. It also lacked fighting gangs, which were already becoming passé when I arrived in Boston in 1958; by the early 1960s they had virtually disappeared, replaced by social clubs loosely modeled on fraternities and sororities formed by social workers or teenagers on their own.

More so among the boys than the girls, the groups were defined by dress: the "block boys" favored knit shirts and sweaters, trousers with no cuffs, sharkskin suits with patterns, dress shirts and thin ties, and sleek tie shoes and Italian-style slip-ons. The "collegiate boys" favored blazers and three-piece suits, button-down and tab-collar shirts with regimental and club ties, corduroy, flannel, and khaki cuffed trousers, penny loafers, saddle shoes and oxfords, and V-neck and crewneck sweaters. This "Ivy" style came to us not by way of Harvard and the other select, predominantly white colleges of New England, but from the Negro colleges, where most Boston black teenagers went to college then. My continuing to dress this way at Harvard led many to assume that I was a prep school alum; one black classmate once said laughingly that I "outprepped the preps."

I felt a member of a fluid teenage society, able to go to a collegiate party one night and party with the block boys the next without changing my style of dress, or worrying that someone was going to "woof" at me for dressing like a college boy—because I knew almost everybody in both crowds. Most everybody did. Black Boston was just too small then for large numbers of teenagers, regardless of their aspirations, not to have known each other for years.

Thus, all through my teen years, Boston's character was leaching into my soul.

But my reasons for wanting to stay at Latin were even

more complex than I could realize then. They also sprang from my developing sense of race.

During those first years in Boston, I had come to understand that most white people despised black people, and that most whites who didn't tolerated those who did. I learned this not through any personal encounters with racism, but from thinking about the white South's violent response to the civil rights movement and looking at what was around me in Boston: blacks were virtually excluded from living in most of the city's blue-collar and middle-class white neighborhoods, and we black youngsters were explicitly warned by parents and older teenagers not to venture into South Boston, the Irish enclave that would be the center of the violent white resistance to the 1974 school desegregation order.

I had been too young to be fully aware of these feelings in elementary school. But I couldn't escape them at the Latin School. There, where fewer than fifty of the two thousand students in the school's six grades in the 1960–61 school year were black, I couldn't avoid recognizing the difference of race, and realizing that I felt inferior.

Outwardly I was carefree that first year—indeed, a bit too carefree. But inwardly I felt confused, different from my white classmates in a way I couldn't articulate because I didn't understand it myself. There weren't any incidents to account for this subtle sense of estrangement; I never encountered anything at the Latin School that smacked of racial prejudice. On the contrary, I would find several teachers who would become my *praeceptores* in the full Latin sense of that word and white classmates whose friendship would endure beyond high school and college.

But that first year I felt that the white students belonged at the Latin School, and I didn't. Yes, there were a few black upperclassmen, but most of the students, all of the faculty, all of the people in the pictures lining the hallway, all of the alumni whose names ringed the top of the auditorium were white. I was black, and it seemed that black people had no history at the Boston Latin School.

That's why the civil rights movement, which had exploded across the South the year I entered Latin, was so important to me. It offered a different perspective on American history, a different answer to the question of why the barriers against African Americans were so fiercely supported by white America.

And the more I learned about that, the more bitter I became. I would see pictures of black boys and men lynched, tarred and feathered, and burned at the stake, or chained to a tree, and I would think: It could have been me; it could have been my father; it could have been my brother. I would watch the television news reports on the demonstrations in the South and silently, fiercely curse white people. Or, reading from the books on black history my brother and I were now obsessively pursuing, I would become so angry that I would start trembling with rage and have to put the book down to calm myself. It was a rage that seemingly knew no limit.

With the anger, however, came a sense of indebtedness, too. I could not have articulated it so, but what I read and saw convinced me that those facing the constant threat of injury and death in the South to challenge the structure of segregation—many of them teenagers like me—were acting on my behalf, that they were making possible the broad opportunities that even then I sensed were becoming available to me.

That sense of obligation, of wanting to be involved in my own liberation, is what led Lloyd and me in the fall of 1963 to the freedom choir of St. John's Episcopal Church in Roxbury. The choir, twenty members strong, was one of several that had been formed in Roxbury that year as a way of involving black school pupils more directly in Boston's school desegregation struggle, a struggle that led to the 1974 federal school desegregation order. Although the choir broke up in 1964 because of the general cooling of civil rights activity in the effort to ensure Lyndon Johnson's election to the presidency, those of us in it remained close throughout high school.

My involvement in the choir furthered my grounding in black Boston. I met a wider circle of teenagers and adults, including two, Melvin Miller, publisher of the *Bay State Banner*, the fledgling black community weekly, and the Reverend Michael

E. Haynes, pastor of Twelfth Baptist Church. They became my tutors in black history and in growing up.

Miller, tall and aristocratic in bearing, had graduated from Latin, Harvard, and Columbia Law School. He had just resigned his post as an assistant state attorney general to establish the *Banner* and would endure years of sacrifice to keep it alive.

Haynes was a graduate of Boston English, Gordon Theological Seminary, and Boston University, and was soon to be elected Boston's (and Massachusetts') first black state representative. He was the more populist-oriented and, having been trained in social work, had been and would continue to be an advisor and "big brother" to scores of Roxbury teenagers.

Outwardly, these two men, both in their thirties, were very different people. But they shared a knowledge of the world beyond Roxbury and a fundamentally intellectual approach to examining it. And they were committed to black people and grounded in the history of black Boston—a knowledge they passed on to me in countless anecdotes.

For example, I learned of Malcolm X, whose years in Boston as Malcolm Little had made him known to many in the black community long before his conversion to the separatist doctrine of the Black Muslims laid the groundwork for his ascent to national fame. I learned that Martin Luther King, Jr., while a graduate theology student at Boston University in the 1950s, had met Coretta Scott, then a graduate student at the New England Conservatory of Music, at Twelfth Baptist, where King was a junior minister along with Haynes. When King decided to return to the South and his destiny, he urged Haynes, who declined, to come with him.

I was fascinated by this information: it helped me understand that becoming educated was an act of affirmation, that it was the key to controlling one's own life.

This understanding of the African American past and present helped turn my thoughts more directly toward college. Having been put back a grade and having then failed a grade, I was one to two years behind my age group. Now, as I saw and heard older friends' travails in applying to college, I realized that what had seemed a disadvantage was actually an advantage. Most of Roxbury's teenagers then applied only to the southern black colleges—in the early 1960s they were virtually the only ones that truly welcomed blacks. But a few, including Lloyd, who would graduate from Latin in 1965, applied only to white colleges in the North. He attended Brandeis University, graduating in 1969.

I had always considered Lloyd more intelligent and more sensible than myself. So his ignoring the interest of several Negro colleges spurred me to think about my own educational future. I wouldn't draw any specific conclusions until late in my junior year. But having seen the disappointment of friends at being rejected by colleges, I knew that I wanted the power to choose or reject to be mine, not the colleges'.

All this led me to realize what my role in the Movement had to be: if my peers in the South were facing physical injury and death, I, from my comfortable perch in the North, would wage the war in the way open to me. I would compete academically against the best white America had to offer, and I would thrive. I would meet the challenge I believed white America posed to every African American: to achieve in the face of its persistent oppression.

The venue in which to do that, of course, was at hand: the Latin School.

But despite my anger at white America and the half-conscious understanding of my responsibility, I was not at war with Boston Latin School. Instead, I was enjoying myself thoroughly there, joking with white classmates, comparing study notes with them, and coming to consider myself an heir to the school's great traditions. I would walk into the auditorium and feel that that very space was hallowed ground, the place where one communed with the shades of the alumni of centuries past, and where they gathered to peer at the current crop of students.

My seriousness about schoolwork burst into the open at the very beginning of sophomore year: I gained approbation with distinction—the reward for honor-level grades and perfect attendance—for the first monthly marking period. It was the first time I had ever gained honors at Latin. Even I was surprised because I hadn't paid any attention to the requirements for approbation and didn't know I was in the running for it. When my homeroom teacher called me to the front of the class to get the small approbation card, I could feel a small shock ripple through the suddenly quiet room. I could almost hear my classmates thinking, "Daniels? Approbation with distinction?" Not that they thought I was stupid. I was sure they didn't think I was stupid. But I was one of the "regular" guys, and even at Latin, the regular guys didn't pay great attention to schoolwork. I felt so proud of myself. From then until I graduated, I became acutely grade-conscious and, though I missed it several times, I pursued approbation every marking period.

I realized that I liked knowing the answers to things. That, I came to understand much later, was affirmation of my ability to be successful, of my very right to exist. And to my surprise I discovered that I found pleasure in working hard, in being tested, in setting goals and bearing down to achieve them, that there was something in me that actually yearned for these challenges. I did immediately relate some of these feelings to my summer of track workouts with a local track club, and for years I would compare getting through a tough assignment to getting through a tough track practice. It was, I would tell myself, as much a matter of preparation, concentration, stamina, and pace as of native intelligence.

My ease in becoming an academic competitor at Latin was furthered by three men. Two were Irish Catholic: Joseph Desmond, my sophomore year Latin teacher, and Wilfred O'-Leary, the school's headmaster; and one, Kenneth Johnson, was African American. Desmond opened my mind to the beauty of the language of classical antiquity and the drama of Roman history. Johnson reworked American history from the dreary subject it was in high school into an exciting, often humorous discussion that emphasized context, not merely facts. Each of them opened my mind to the joy and power of intellectual achievement, and my newfound sense of purpose meshed perfectly with O'Leary's efforts to increase the school's academic rigor and its reputation, both of which had slipped during the previous headmaster's tenure. O'Leary's goal was to foster in us the expectation of achieving and a felt obligation to achieve.

His stern, ruddy visage set off by a shock of snow-white hair, O'Leary looked and acted the archetypal prep-school headmaster—autocratic toward the faculty but solicitous toward the students, especially the upperclassmen, and particularly the more prominent juniors and seniors. I became one of them. This was partly due to my being black. My ten black classmates and I were the largest group of African Americans ever to reach Latin's upper grades in one class, and O'Leary made a concerted—and successful—effort to see that we all graduated. And it was also because I had squeezed into the top quarter of our 260-member class by the middle of junior year. This qualified me for membership in the school's chapter of the National Honor Society.

At the induction ceremonies later that spring O'Leary forcefully "suggested" to my beaming mother that I had decided where I wanted to go to college.

"It's Harvard, isn't it," he said evenly, smiling at her. "Well, I don't know, sir," I answered truthfully. He became mock-serious as his eyes locked on mine. "Lee, you do want to attend Harvard, don't you." I understood it was not a question. "Oh, yes, sir," I replied. "I want to go to Harvard." Smiling broadly once again, he winked at my mother, whose face was now suffused with radiance, said "Good, I'm glad you decided that," and strolled away to greet other students and their families.

Before that encounter I hadn't yet considered any particular college; afterward, there was no other college I thought of.

What happened to me during my teen years, seemed to constitute a paradox: as I became more racially conscious, more unforgiving toward white America, I also came to cherish the predominantly white Latin School and to regard myself as an heir to its most deeply held traditions. I don't think I could have then reconciled my growing race-related bitterness with my deepening attraction to a school that enshrined the "white" values of classicism. Nor did I try to, although I was dimly aware that by daily challenging my every inclination to classify all whites as my enemies, white friends and teachers were preventing me from being consumed by rage. I accepted as a given that I lived in two worlds that were supposedly incompatible. I accepted the necessity of learning to judge and think and feel in two colors. Much later I would realize that for African Americans, life is a continual process of negotiating the indifferent or hostile forces arrayed against us, and that we need to find a way to look forward to it, to engage in the struggle and take energy from it.

# DINNERTIME

## Helen Epstein

HELEN EPSTEIN was born in Prague, Czechoslovakia in 1947 and emigrated to New York City with her parents after the Communist takeover of that country the following year. She grew up on the West Side of Manhattan, where her parents—both concentration camp survivors—were part of the city's Czech emigré community. She attended Hunter College High School. In college, Epstein worked as a part-time journalist and began writing about her experiences as a child of Holocaust survivors. Her book *Children of the Holocaust* examines her own life and the lives of other children of concentration-camp survivors. She has written three other books: *Music Talks*, *The Companies She Keeps*, and *Joe Papp: An American Life*. Helen Epstein now lives in Massachusetts with her husband and two sons.

At five-thirty, when her girls had swept up and gone home, my mother sat alone in her workroom and lit the sixteenth or seventeenth cigarette of the day. She leaned her head on her open palm and stared out at the dim stone apartment houses on either side of Sixty-seventh Street; a few moments in the only corner of our apartment that was her own. Shelves of old shoe boxes formed the boundary with the living room where she and my father slept at night. They were filled with buttons and zippers, sequins, elastic bands, metal snaps and artificial flowers, all labeled in my mother's illegible script. Beside them was fabric: satins, wools, organzas and glittering brocade for the customers from Palm Beach. Her dummy stood in the center of the room near the old Singer sewing machine that had been her first big purchase in the United States. Some of her Prague customers had preceded her to New York. She had started working right away.

My mother looked up at the portrait she had framed in leather and hung over her cutting table. It was an old photograph, sepia-toned, of a woman's face. A dark fur collar rested against her cheek and made her skin seem very white. She had dark hair, firm eyebrows and sad, glistening eyes.

"Who's that?" I asked when I was three.

"That's Pepi," said my mother. "Grandmother Pepi."

"Where is she?"

"She died. She was killed."

"Was she bad?"

My mother was startled. "No. It was the Germans who were bad. Very bad."

"Where is she?"

"I told you she died," my mother said. "I don't know where she died. The Germans didn't tell me. Now let me do some work."

My mother's eyes were like my grandmother's: dark brown, so deep with secrets that they seemed to have no bottom when you looked into them. They were seductive eyes that drew you in and made you want to know who she was.

"Why did the Germans kill her?"

My mother did not know how to answer me. How did other parents explain? Why did this child never stop asking questions? One after another: Who put the number on your arm? Why do you keep it? Why won't it come off? Did it hurt when they put it on? Why doesn't Daddy have one?

My mother worried about the questions and, with my father, about the answers. My parents had determined not to frighten me with their recollections, yet they did not want to lie. They had not anticipated the extent of a child's curiosity, just as they had not expected the commotion that my younger brother and I could make.

"*Mommy!*" I would scream into the workroom. "Tommy's hitting me!"

"I am not!" my brother called in after me.

My mother sighed, put out her cigarette, and stood up as the two of us ran into the workroom. She worried about our constant squabbling almost as much as about my questions. She did not know much about children. She herself had been an only child, whose closest friend had been my grandmother Pepi. At the age of fifteen, after French and German schools, she had quit to join her mother's business. It was a salon for *haute couture* in the center of Prague, with thirty girls in the workroom and a cosmopolitan clientele. My mother remembered railway carriages, seasonal trips to Paris and Berlin to purchase fabrics and view the new collections. There were long walks with her mother and afternoon tea dances in smart hotels.

In New York, my mother chose styles and fabrics from the pages of *Vogue*, *L'Officiel* and *Bazaar*. Only two girls sewed in her workroom and in summer, when her customers went off to Connecticut or Long Island, my mother sat in her workroom alone.

By five-thirty, her features were slack, her eyes bleary from following the movements of her needle. Although her hair was a deep brown and her cheeks dimpled girlishly when she smiled, my mother looked older than thirty-five. She often sat alone, in the half-dark room, sewing; that is my earliest memory of her. She appeared stunned by solitude. As I looked up at her, she seemed to be behind a pane of glass.

When she wasn't working, my mother would read or spend three hours listening to the Saturday afternoon Texaco Opera House, but I rarely saw my mother having fun. My father was chronically unemployed, so most of the time, she sewed. She made coats and suits for Mrs. Lewis, Mrs. Chauncey, Mrs. Glucken and the other women who sat down on my parents' beds in the living room, flipping the pages of glossy magazines, weighing the possibilities of necklines and hemlines, for the most part uncurious about who she was and where she came from. For them, she was a great find, a refugee, a good dressmaker with hands, they said, of gold.

Her customers in Prague, my mother said, had been

cultured people. In America they were, for the most part, neither aristocratic nor gracious. Most paid their bills in due course—although one woman had run off to the Yucatán owing my mother eight hundred dollars—but few appreciated her patience with them. They prattled on about their husbands and lovers, the deteriorating quality of help in St. Thomas, the difficulties of finding hats and shoes to match their dresses. Occasionally, they forgot who my mother was and complained that New York was being "overrun by refugees" or that a certain stockbroker had attempted to "Jew us down." My mother would remain impassive. We would hear about it at dinner. The next day, there would be a telephone apology or perhaps a pair of gloves from Saks. My mother did not allow what she called "scenes" to develop between herself and her customers. She let them play patron, and when they invited her to the theater or to the opera, she went. The customers' checks paid our rent. The customer, however self-indulgent, troublesome or offensive, was life.

By five-thirty though, when my brother and I came tearing into the workroom, her reserves of patience were spent. She threatened, and sometimes delivered, quick slaps that stung. Then she dispatched my brother to his room and me to the kitchen. Dinner was at six and could not be delayed. The notion that one might take a nap beforehand, or drink cocktails, or simply do nothing for an hour had no currency with my parents. As six o'clock approached, a tension was palpable in our household. It was like the anxiety of travelers on their way to an airport or railway station. If they are late, if their watches have stopped or if they have misread the schedule, they will be left behind.

While I set the kitchen table, my mother stood beside the stove, cutting up potatoes and preparing meat. She lit more cigarettes, stopped to touch a hand to the small of her back, or gasped slightly when she left her weight on one leg for too long and it froze into a cramp beneath her. She had been injured in concentration camp when a roof collapsed on her back and since then she complained of a slipped disk. Sometimes, when she moved uncomfortably around the kitchen, my mother said she had colitis. Or a migraine. Or a muscle spasm. Or melancholia.

The women in our family had all suffered from that, she said. My great-grandmother had jumped from a third-story window and died.

Her pain was visible. It drained the blood from her skin, making her appear even paler than she normally was, and the blue numbers tattooed on her forearm almost seemed to blaze. I watched her as I folded napkins, brought out glasses and silverware and plates. I could see the pain creep through her body, trapped, moving from place to place, eluding a list of specialists which grew longer each year. Internists, neurologists, osteopaths, chiropractors, even hypnotists had treated my mother. They put her in traction, prescribed lotions, pills, injections, exercises, diets. But the pain would not go away. At times, when she read or listened to music or when we were in the country and my father and she relaxed together, it would ebb. But then, without warning, triggered by an innocent motion of an arm or leg, it would return. "Don't just stand there like an idiot! Help me sit down!" she would order, in a tense, distorted voice. Or worse, she would say nothing. She would gasp and remain in the position in which pain had cast her, her eyes like wounds.

I would stop what I was doing, offer my arm, draw up something on which she could sit. I had no idea what was happening to her when she became stuck in space, unable to budge. I was seven years old, loud, impertinent, active, all the things my parents meant when they said, "American child." The fact that my mother, who had lost her menstrual period for three years during the war, could produce such a healthy child still seemed somewhat of a miracle to her. Cousins in America had sent monthly packages of powdered milk for me to Prague like deposits in a bank of new life. In New York, I was plied with food, books, art, music and dancing lessons; I was taken skating, skiing, bicycle riding; to the opera, to concerts, to the theater—all on a budget that barely sufficed to pay the rent. Her child was more than a leaf in the future for my mother. I could recapture the best of her past.

We talked as I set the table. That is, I chattered on about my penmanship and arithmetic grades, our class spelling bees, our trips to museums and candy factories. I told jokes: "Mommy? Why did the moron salute the refrigerator?"

"Why did the moron salute . . ." my mother repeated in her sharply accented English. "I don't know. Why?"

"Because it was General Electric!" I sang out. "Why did the moron throw the clock from the Empire State Building?"

"I don't know."

"Because he wanted to see time *fly!*

"*Hhhhmmpphh!*" said my mother.

"Do you want to hear another one?"

"Later," she told me in Czech, going about her business with an intentness I never saw in other mothers. Her motions were measured, intensely concentrated. Sometimes, if she had had a good day, she laughed at my stories from school but mostly she told me to quit fooling around or else the table wouldn't be ready when my father got home.

My father came home ravenous, as if he had not eaten in several days when, in fact, he ate three big meals every day without fail. He was fifty-one years old, a tall, strong, optimistic man with the broad shoulders and tapered hips of a swimmer. His forehead was high, his eyes lively under tangled brows. In Prague, he had been a water polo player and a long-standing member of the Czechoslovak National Olympic Committee. He had retained the carriage of a man who lived an athlete's regimen long after retiring from competition. *In mens sana in corpore sano,* he intoned in the mornings when he woke us up at seven, wet from his cold shower, a towel wrapped loosely around his waist. He was sixteen years older than my mother, a man who had commanded the best tables in Prague restaurants, who now could not find a job.

Upon their arrival in New York in 1948, my father had walked over to the New York Athletic Club on Central Park South. He believed firmly in the equality conferred by sport. He had participated in the Berlin Olympics in 1936 where "the American Negro Jesse Owens," as he called him, had won a gold medal. The New York Athletic Club would surely help him find work as a swim coach, he thought. My mother and he were invited to view one water polo game there but the reception they received was markedly cool. My father spoke little English and it was only after a few days that someone explained to him that the club was restricted, closed to Jews.

My father moved from job to job. He worked as a shipping clerk, a salesman, a bookkeeper. Finally, a neighbor whose husband had died taught him how to use the cutting machine that the couple had used in their T-shirt business. He became a cutter in the garment center, working for other refugees. Each evening he came home tired from the scrap-strewn factories of Seventh Avenue, irritated by the filth and rudeness of the subways. He strode into the apartment with a mangled copy of the *New York Post* under his arm, kissed my mother good evening, and then stood for a moment, tying up traffic in the small kitchen.

"What's for dinner?" he asked in Czech and, without waiting for an answer, pulled open the refrigerator door, found an open can of sardines or an end of salami and wolfed down the food, using a piece of bread as a fork. He stood this way, hunched over the kitchen counter in his overcoat, for several moments. Then, sated, he turned to us with one of his daily garment center anecdotes, offering me a taste of salami.

"For heaven's sake, Kurt," my mother interrupted him. "Dinner will be on the table in a few minutes."

"I'm hungry. I worked all day," replied my father, chewing hard, as if to intimate that were he deprived of this snack he might very well drop dead right there on the kitchen floor, famished.

My mother said nothing. She lit another cigarette, pushed the rings of salami that lay strewn about the kitchen counter into a small pile, and threw them into the garbage pail. My father asked me what I had done in school, whether I had done well in the spelling bee. We were learning to spell together: I at school, he in the night classes he attended to learn English. He came home with passages from Shakespeare, homilies and proverbs which he recited with one hand on his chest like Napoleon, chin thrust forward. His pronunciation of the syllables was so distorted that the sense of what he was saying got lost. "*Ehr*-ly to *bed*," he intoned, "*Ehr*-ly to *rise*. Makes the man *heal*-thy, *weal*-thy and *wise*."

"Tommy! Are you washing your hands?" called my mother.

"Was there any mail?" asked my father. He meant: had any checks from a customer come in?

My mother shook her head and took out the meat. We ate cold cuts for breakfast, leftover meat for lunch and roast or stew or chops for dinner. When I asked why we never had tuna casserole like other people, my mother said they had gone three years without meat and that was enough. The kind in the supermarket did not pass muster. My mother shopped at the Nevada Meat Market whose owners had noted her blue tattoo and extended credit when she had no money to pay for her purchases.

Her tattoo was like a mysterious flag. It made some people blush, turn their eyes aside, mumble odd, garbled things. Others acted as if my mother was a species of saint. I watched her respond to both groups with a fierce pride. Her manner, always abrupt, became distant. She threw up a wall between herself and them.

"Tommy! Dinner!" she called now, like a train conductor.

My brother was preoccupied with trucks, trains and elevators. He was four years old, thin and unenthusiastic about meals. He fidgeted in his chair and pushed his food in circles around a central morsel on his plate, making my mother even more nervous. In a small voice, he asked for chocolate milk, but most of the time he kept quiet, especially at mealtimes when tensions were high.

My father was already at the table, hunched, head down. He swallowed his food so quickly that he seemed not to chew, looking up only to see what my mother was doing, why she hadn't sat down to the table herself.

"Daddy didn't always eat this way," my mother sometimes told me. "His family had manners. They had a cook and servants." My father himself did not acknowledge any peculiarity in his eating habits. "When someone sits down to eat, he should eat and do nothing else," he said. "That's the trouble in America. Everyone wants to sit with one fanny on three stools. They want to watch television while they eat. They want to read a book. They want to conduct a debate!" By the time my mother had finished dressing the salad and sat down with us, his plate was clean. He never left a trace of food, not even a streak of gravy.

My mother sat down and served herself.

"Daddy?" I said.

"What?" He wiped his chin.

"You're finished and nobody else has started yet."

He glanced at my mother.

"Don't be fresh to your father," she said automatically. She took my brother's plate and began to cut up the meat on it in brisk strokes. Her face looked swollen, the way it did before she started to cry. My brother looked down at the table top. There was silence in the kitchen.

My father took another helping of meat but we could sense an explosion coming. It did not take much for my father to be drawn into conflict. Almost every evening when he came home from work, he announced that he had severed relations with someone in the garment district. A waiter had served him lukewarm soup. A fellow cutter had made an insulting remark about refugees. "And you, Izzy?" my father replied. "Was your father an Indian chief?"

Even his boss was not exempt from my father's chronic rages. Also a refugee, who had escaped from the Warsaw Ghetto, this man capitalized on my father's status. He paid substandard wages and could offer no guarantee of employment, but he understood that my father needed to be left alone to do his work, that he had difficulty accepting authority. My father carted fabric, rolled it out on long narrow tables until it was six or seven inches thick and then sliced through the wad with a two-inch, razor-sharp blade. There were times when his thoughts strayed from the blouse and apron pieces beneath him to the Olympic Games or to the small town where he was born when Franz Josef was still Emperor, and the blade sheared off a piece of his skin and flesh with the cheap cloth. He came home with a bandage enlarging his hand. After dinner, he took it off to show us that he had not lost his finger, that it had stopped bleeding, that he was all right.

The garment center was a relatively safe place for my father. He could lose his temper daily, rail in broken English at his colleagues and risk nothing more than a harangue in return. In the Seventh Avenue luncheonettes near his place of work, he was known to the waitresses as Mr. Epstein, the gentleman from Prague. He saluted the elevator operator in the morning and greeted the receptionist with a deference he had learned from his father. His style was Austro-Hungarian, circa 1910.

Although we had no sense, not even a sketch, of where he came from, my father expected that we behave as children did in Roudnice-nad-Labem. That meant waiting at the door when he came home from work, our hair brushed behind our ears, hands and faces clean, attitude smiling but subdued. We would say, "Good evening, Daddy," eat our dinners, have our baths, and go off to bed. The fact that my mother, who did not enjoy the services of servants as his mother had, was exhausted by dinnertime was a mystery to him.

Since he had been separated from his family in the Terezin Ghetto, he had idealized his mother as well as the general tenor of family life. He had named me after her and when I did not conform to this model I had never seen, he was perplexed and, sometimes, sad. "How *can* you whistle before breakfast?" he would ask me. "Grandmother Helena never did that. Don't you know young ladies don't whistle? You'll marry a crazy husband!"

His expectations, the frustrations of his life in a closed-in, poorly ventilated factory, and our behavior often collided. When he was tired, when his optimism was worn down by worries about money or my mother's health, a terrible anger erupted from him. His face grew dark and when he began to shout, his fury was like a sudden hailstorm.

It was utterly silent at the dinner table. My mother began to eat. I ate. But my brother let the food sit on his plate. His mouth, which was not as clean as my father would have wished, hung open as he looked at the ceiling, then down at the floor between his legs. He played with his fork and when the fork hit his glass of chocolate milk, it made a small *ping!*

My father looked up. He took a breath and his chest grew even larger than it was; his shoulders loomed over the table. "Tell me, what are you waiting for?" he demanded. "You think food stays warm forever? Or you are too fine to eat this kind of meat? Perhaps you would like some filet mignon?"

My brother's eyes grew larger as the volume of my father's voice rose, the Czech interspersed with a coarse German whose meaning we deduced rather than understood. "*Hajzel!*" he shouted. "*Svine!*" The words meant "toilet" and "swine." He seemed to be in another world, raging at people we could not see. Our misbehavior was just a trigger that released a rage which was there all the time, locked inside like my mother's pain. Once unlocked, it spurted out of him lavalike and furious, impossible to restrain.

"Don't stare at me like an idiot! Eat!"

"Kurt, *stop* it," came my mother's voice, also in Czech, terribly low and yet sharp.

"Spoiled brats!" my father muttered and there was a second of quiet.

My brother dropped his fork, splattering gravy on the table.

"Pigs! You eat like pigs in a pigsty—not like children from a good family! You should be grateful you have meat to eat and instead you poke around your plate. Brats! Miserable brats! Do you know what we would have given for a meal like this! Seven hundred calories a day we were given! And we didn't spend the day in school!"

"*Kurt!*" my mother said.

"Don't interrupt me. When—"

"I can't *stand* this anymore," my mother shouted over his voice. "*Always* at dinner! We cannot have *one* peaceful dinner in this household! We *have* to have a scene. You can't live a day of your life without getting mad!"

She too looked gripped by something that had nothing to do with us at the dinner table in our kitchen in New York. Her jaw went rigid, her eyes were rimmed with red. She gasped as a pain caught her back. Then she burst into sobs and ran out of the kitchen.

My brother and I sat still. We listened to the shuffle of my mother's steps as she ran into the bathroom, closed the door and locked it. My father went to the sink for a glass of water. He drank it there, then began to pace between the table and the stove.

"Eat!" he ordered. "Or do you want a slap in the face?"

My father found nothing incongruous in this demand, just as he found it perfectly natural to become angry whenever my brother or I hurt ourselves. Anything that endangered the health of his children was a personal threat and the fact that we were not eating was no exception. But I did not understand this then. I hated my father when he lost his temper. He spoiled dinner, he made my mother cry, he insulted us with ugly names. He was a bully.

I did not say this out loud. I was afraid he would hit me, and also I knew that when he was in this state he understood nothing one told him. The only thing to do was wait until my father's rage had run its course. My brother retreated whenever this was happening. His pale eyes and face, his blond hair, seemed to melt into the yellow wall behind him. His expression was bleak and closed. I never knew what he was thinking. Unlike me, he could not even pretend to eat.

"To your room!" my father ordered.

My brother froze, fork in hand, like a small, stunned animal. Then he slipped down from his chair and out of the kitchen, glad to have escaped a thrashing.

My father too left the kitchen. He walked to his desk in the living room and switched on the small lamp over his work space. Within minutes he was absorbed in the large black ledger of my mother's business, paying bills, writing out sums in his fine, graceful hand. He made small, deft marks in the book, furrowing his forehead so that it became a steeplechase of lines. If you had asked him then why the house was so quiet, why everyone had taken refuge, he would have been unable to say. For him, the storm was over.

For me, the frightening part had just begun. The silence was like a great big open hole I could fall into if I wasn't careful. My father often got lost this way. He would stop in the middle of a sentence and his eyes would go vague. His lower lip dropped and he was unreachable. I'd tap his shoulder or call his name without success. I was sure he was in that brown-toned world of photographs, among all the people who lived in the yellow envelope in his desk.

My mother did not move from world to world so easily. Her exits and entrances were theatrical, jarring and full of suppressed feeling. All the rage my father spent on taxicab drivers, bank tellers and other people who did not treat him with appropriate respect, my mother turned inward. It festered inside her and came out only when she barricaded herself in the bathroom for hours, carrying on a broken conversation with me through the closed door.

That was where I stationed myself after an explosion, with excuses for opening a conversation, disguises for my need of reassurance.

"Mommy? I need someone to test me for the social studies quiz tomorrow," or "Mommy? The refrigerator's leaking." My mother was the parent who fixed things. In Auschwitz, during the selection of prisoners for work or death, she had identified herself as an electrician rather than a dressmaker. She had survived by pretending to know how to repair faulty wiring, and had become so good at it that now she rarely needed to call a repairman.

"Mommy?"

She did not answer. There was no sound behind the locked door. Behind it was a medicine cabinet. It was crammed full of pill bottles, tubes, yellowing prescription labels and a few hypodermic needles that a doctor had given her. My mother knew her pills by sight. I knew them as well as I knew the candy bars at the pharmacy where I was sent every week. There was Darvon. Morphine. Butazolidin. The pharmacist, like our butcher, extended us credit.

"Mommy?" I touched the door with my knuckles.

"Leave me alone. I want to be alone."

"Are you okay?"

My mother was crying. "I don't want to go on anymore. I can't stand it."

I listened hard. I thought I could somehow leach the pain from her by listening. It would leave her body, enter mine, and be lessened by sharing. Otherwise, I thought, it would one day kill my mother. She could kill herself easily behind the locked door. She could give herself an injection or swallow a bottleful of pills as I stood waiting outside.

"Mommy!"

No reply.

It was nearly eight o'clock by now and I went into the living room where my father had dozed off. Sometimes when my mother locked herself in the bathroom, he insisted that he needed to use it. Once he had threatened to call the Fire Department to get her out of there. But when he figured that the situation was under control, he simply went to sleep. I did not understand that then. All I knew was that my mother was gone, and that she might disappear the way she said her own parents had, without notice, without any noise.

"Mommy!" I banged on the door.

"What? What do you want?"

It was not a real question but it was all I needed for the moment. My brother was inside the hall closet, playing elevator with its sliding doors.

"Going up?" he asked quietly. "Fifth floor?"

Then he closed the closet door, waited, and let the people out.

I went into my mother's workroom where I could make believe that behind the shoeboxes of ribbons and zippers were secret panels, doors and cupboards. In that room, in the dark, I could be Nancy Drew or the Hardy Boys. Her workroom was my attic and it contained secret messages from the past to be discovered in treasure chests, old hats and tablecloths. Downstairs, in their prim sitting room, would be my grandparents. My grandfather would sit in his socks and smoke a pipe and say what my father had really been like when he was small. My grandmother Helena would tell me it was all right, sometimes, to whistle. But I could not imagine very well what they wore, how they talked, or how they would act toward me. The brown-colored photographs distanced them in time, and the one-line phrases in which my father described them were so general that I had no idea what they were really like.

My grandmother Pepi was different. Her photograph over my mother's cutting table was even prettier at night. Her eyes glowed. I did not believe she was dead. She did not look old enough to die and it made no sense, what my mother said, that the Germans had shot her. She was never tired like my mother or likely to flare into a rage. Her eyes were like a caress. Her lips looked about to form a word. I wondered where she was and when she would come back. My mother said she was not buried. No one had been buried. One day, I thought, my grandmother Pepi would step out of her photograph and into the room, like the fairy godmothers in storybooks. She would come live with us and my mother would not be so lonely then.

I went back to the bathroom and knocked.

"What is it?" My mother's voice was clear now, not muffled with crying.

"Are you okay?"

"I'm okay. I'm just depressed."

"Are you coming out?"

"I'll be out in a little while. Go get ready for bed. Help Tommy undress."

I did not move away.

"Don't worry. I'm okay. I just want to be alone a little bit more."

I pulled my little brother out of the hall closet and told him to get ready for bed. Then I went into the kitchen and cleared the table. Putting things in order was my way of pretending that nothing was wrong. It was the tactic I often used to ward away pain. There was no way I could shout back at my father; no way I could reproach my mother. How could I not be a happy, healthy, good girl after all they had been through? My father got angry when he saw me listless or unhappy, just as he got angry when my brother or I fell down and scraped our knees. "After the war I put three things what were most important to me," my father would tell people. "First freedom. Then health. And the third thing, contentment. I wanted that my child will live in a free country without any experience what I had to suffer."

I did not like to hear my father say these things. He said them all the time, to anyone who would listen. He talked in a loud, emphatic voice, in an English so queerly cadenced that it sounded as though he were speaking Czech. I did not want to know that my father had been in prison, that other men had spit on him, kicked him, beat him. He did not mention these things but we knew them nonetheless. The way his feet looked, the toes yellowing, the nails deformed; the way he ate meals; the way he reacted to demands on him—all said more than words. How could my father, so tall, so strong, let that happen? And how could he tell people about it?

"When we came to Auschwitz," my father would say, "we went out of the trains and I was marching toward Dr. Mengele, who was making a selection. He asked sometimes questions and said, 'right,' 'left,' but we didn't know what it meant. When I stood before him, he asked me a question: '*Sind Sie wirklich gesund?*' Are you really healthy? Because I was after a sickness and I was looking in bad shape, especially I was not shaven for three days. I said, '*Jawohl!*' Yes! and he sent me to the good side. From fifteen hundred people were saved three hundred. So I passed the first test. After twenty minutes we went to a barrack where a young SS officer came and asked people who wanted to volunteer for work. Most of my friends joined these groups. I also, but in the last second something came to my mind and I stepped aside. There were three groups. The first went to the mines and nobody came back. The third group nobody came back. The second group, what I joined, ninety-six people came back. So you see . . ."

My father would smile, showing teeth that also reflected the years of the war. "I was thinking all my life what was it, was this a sixth sense, was this God, was this a providence? Because the fact that I am here and can give you this report is a matter of one fraction of a second what I decided."

I went into the living room to kiss my father good night, and then joined my brother in the bedroom we shared. I lay awake listening for the sound of the bathroom door. The apartment was silent. Outside, there was a long wail of police sirens.

By the time my mother finally came in to say good night, I pretended to be sleeping. I could throw up my own walls. I could make her wait.

"Are you awake?" she asked.

I did not answer.

"You know Daddy doesn't really mean anything when he shouts like that," she said. "You know he loves you."

She did not volunteer any explanation of her own behavior, as if there were nothing at all peculiar about locking herself in the bathroom for two hours. Nothing she said acknowledged that she had, in fact, done so. Any reference I might make to it would be a reproach and I could not reproach my mother. I knew the stories. She was doing the best she could. Even to compare her to other mothers was treason.

But when she left the bedroom, I did. I imagined other mothers, other dinner tables with white tablecloths and decorum, where families conversed quietly and nothing went wrong. I imagined other fathers, who had offices where they were doctors or lawyers who did not feel compelled to challenge every parking attendant who told them where to leave their car. At their homes, I was sure, these things did not happen. Children misbehaved, mothers and fathers quarreled but there was no extra presence in the air like there was in our home.

In our home words ricocheted between worlds, their meaning uncertain. My parents told stories but the stories never explained. They talked about people, but the people were all gone. Simple facts required long explanations. Few things could be taken for granted starting with the fact that we were, all of us, alive.

I could hear my mother in the living room getting ready

for bed. My father was already asleep; every few minutes I could hear him snore. After a while, the light in the living room went out. The apartment was completely dark. I fell asleep.

In the morning, my father was wet from his shower, dripping water on the floor, his eyes fresh and happy. If he was feeling especially cheerful, he whistled Reveille and if my brother and I did not have our feet on the floor right away he left and came back with a wet washcloth which he wrung gleefully over our heads. There was struggling and laughter, a scrambling to start a new day.

In the kitchen, my mother had already prepared breakfast. She was brisk and efficient in the morning, despite the stiffness in her back. She wrapped sandwiches in wax paper, sorted out our clothing and hauled me off to brush and plait my hair into two sturdy braids. She was better than other mothers because she did five things at once as if they were nothing. Her face was so vivid, her eyes so busy with thoughts of the day ahead that I forgot the emptiness that had been in them the night before. There was nothing wrong with my mother in the morning. She did not need help. She did not question her right to be alive.

In the mornings when I went to school I had no questions either. I did not wonder why good people got killed or were put in prison when they had done nothing wrong. I did not wonder why we had no money when, before, my parents had had plenty of it. I did not wonder about the place they had come from or why they had had to leave it.

I kissed my mother good-bye, clutched my Lone Ranger lunchbox and set off for school. I ran races during recess and sang songs from Broadway musicals during show-and-tell. I was Peter Pan and Cinderella and a Mickey Mouse Club Mouseketeer. In school, we learned about government and science, things which had reasons and unshakeable order. In arithmetic, grammar and gym, it was easy to push away the things I saw and heard and imagined the night before. I must have imagined it all, I thought. No one else talked about such things. They were not in the books I read or in the world I lived in. They had not happened. I refused to believe they had happened at all.

# ABSOLUTELY SOMEDAY

Tracy Marx

TRACY MARX was born in New York City and grew up in Connecticut. Although her mother was born in Poland, Marx never learned to speak Polish because in her family it was always reserved for confidential "grownup" conversation. Currently, Marx is a Writer-in-the-College at the Eugene Lang College of the New School for Social Research and works at a New York City publishing house. She is also pursuing her M.A. in writing at The City College of New York. Like her mother in "Absolutely Someday," Tracy Marx now speaks to her grandmother on the telephone almost every day. "Absolutely Someday" is her first published piece.

Many mornings I am awakened too early by reports of the latest family drama, usually involving my eighty-year-old grandmother who lives about fifteen hundred miles away. These complaints come from my mother who stands in front of the window outside my bedroom door applying makeup before a small, round mirror that rests atop the air conditioner ledge. The tirade is like a soap opera that begins at about seven-thirty A.M., except that I can't turn it off.

Usually I bury myself under the covers, hoping to muffle her words, her Polish-accented shrieks of disbelief at "the nerve, the gall, the utter senility" of my grandmother. I can see my mother's eyebrows bob up and down as she tweezes them between adjectives. Grandma is usually guilty of nothing more serious than forgetting the exact details of a piece of family gossip, or of advising someone to put too much spice in a soup. But my mother is, you see, a very dramatic woman. Well, we say dramatic. Others call her high strung, even neurotic.

"Please let me sleep," I plead.

"Okay, I'm sorry," she answers, but continues. I groan a little, snore loudly, sigh deeply. Nothing helps. Finally I tell her that she is upsetting me, that I will grow up with many tension-related problems, and most of all that I will become hopelessly neurotic, just like her.

"Everyone is neurotic," is my mother's reply. "Not everyone is psychotic. Psychotic is what you must watch out for."

She applies her powder a bit more violently. "I am by no means psychotic. And neither are you," she will say, approaching my bed with lipstick poised, adding this last point while peering deep into my eyes that peer back at her from beneath the covers.

I think actually that she is phobic. I think she has matriphobia, which is not a fear of mattresses as you might imagine, but a fear of becoming just like one's mother. I found it in the dictionary. I knew it must be some kind of a fear because I've heard about a distant cousin named Gabriella who is claustrophobic, which means she is afraid of closed-in places. This I can understand. But this other kind of fear I'm not so sure of. I mean, my mother does embarrass me sometimes, maybe many times, like every Sunday when we sing in church and she sings so loud I swear it feels as if hers is the only voice in the whole congregation. But still, I wouldn't mind being like her.

"What is your mother? Bulgarian?" my friend Bobby asked once after he called my house and my mother answered the telephone. Bobby never listens to the homework assignment at school, so he always has to call someone to get it.

"No," I say, a little insulted. The word *Bulgarian*, the way he said it, has such a clunky, clumsy sound—nothing at all like my graceful, elegant mother. "She is Polish."

I prepare myself for the list of Polack jokes this information usually unleashes. If only someone would think up some new ones.

Actually, we like these jokes, my mother and I. Our favorite is the one about the ice cubes. Maybe you know it. It goes like this: "Why aren't there any ice cubes in Poland? Because they lost the recipe!" We're just as willing to laugh at the other ones too, but they're usually not so funny. And the ice-cube joke is one of the few not shared by the Italians, Chinese, Russians, or any of the other people who are always joked about, which come to think of it is just about everybody. My mother doesn't understand why on television she always hears people say *Polack* as if it were an insult.

"A Polack is what a Polish person *is*. It is what Polish people call each other," she explained to me. This has proved a good thing to know.

Until people started asking me about it, I was never even aware of my mother having an accent. Except when it comes to *v*s and *w*s, that is. For example, the other day we went to buy me a vest and my mother asked the sales lady where the "wests" were. This means that she has been thinking *north, south, east, vest.*

"Go west, young man!" I shouted, hoping it would help her remember. She also has some trouble with *th*s because there is no such sound in Polish. And once she said she had to call the plumber and she pronounced the *b*. It took me a long time to convince her that you aren't supposed to pronounce it, even though it's there.

"A ridiculous language," she muttered.

The things that show she didn't grow up in America are not in the sounds she makes (except when she imitates a dog barking—to her it is more like "how-how" than "woof-woof"), but in the foods she likes, the sausagey smells that come from my brown bag when I bring my lunch to school, the kasha and the beets that we eat, and the pierogi, for example.

"What are these?" Bobby asks one night, when he and my sort-of friend Ginny have dinner at my house.

"They're called pierogi and I think you will not find them so strange after you try one," my mother says. She has seen this before.

"Oh, ravioli!" Bobby says with surprise after cutting into

one of the steaming noodle pockets on his plate, and seeing the warm potato-cheese filling ooze into the nearby dollops of sour cream and applesauce.

"Yeah," Ginny agrees, cutting into one of hers that is stuffed with cabbage and mushrooms. "These are like some dumplings I had at the Chinese restaurant last week."

"That's right," my mother says. "Every country seems to have its version of the same thing."

Each pierogi is like a little surprise. In some there are meat or just plain potatoes. We start playing a guessing game with them while we eat.

"Yes please or no thank you?" Ginny asks, passing the salt to me, as if to teach me manners. She does things like that a lot, which is why I think of her only as my sort-of friend. I'm still deciding how much I really like her. Like in morning chapel at school, if any of us are turning and whispering to each other she puts that finger to her lips that means "hush up," and she makes that circular motion in the air with her other index finger that means "turn your head back around," just like the teachers do.

"No thanks, teacher," I say a little snottily, ignoring the salt. My mother refills my glass of milk and makes those little clucking noises with her tongue that mean "Now, now, be calm." But she does this very quietly. I think she's also still deciding how much she likes Ginny.

For dessert we have ice cream and also those Rice Krispies marshmallow treat things that my mother likes to make. Very American. Personally, I hate marshmallow anything. But she makes these more for herself than for anyone else. My mother loves Rice Krispies cereal. She says it is the first thing she ate in America.

My mother also loves mayonnaise. "What is this delicacy?" she thought the first time she tasted it. She has found a hundred different ways to use it. I think she is obsessed with mayonnaise, even though it's been many years since she came to America.

It's been many years since she saw the big farm where

she grew up, with its horses and pigs, and the many relatives who lived there too, or since she ran around and around the big chestnut tree with its bench that circled the entire trunk. She tells me how they used to pick fallen chestnuts for stringing in the winter. It's been a long time since she tasted "real" cherries. She says I don't know what real cherries taste like. "Warm and sweet, like heaven," she says.

I think she should go back to Poland and visit. But she says there is no one there she would know anymore, no one who would know her. But I would still want to visit if I were she. I think it would make her happy. She says it would only make her sad. She says that someday I will understand. That's what all parents say, I tell her. Very original. "Then I guess I am all parents," she answers breezily, knowing that is far from true. But then when she is really angry or upset (I can always tell because her nostrils flare), like when I nag her to take me to the movies even though she is too tired, or to buy me something we can't really afford, then she says that I don't understand and that she hopes I never have to.

Sometimes it's hard to imagine my mother, who always takes the elevator in our apartment building, living on a farm with chickens and cows, and riding a bicycle everywhere, even though we have photographs to prove it. It's hard to imagine her in a world without Rice Krispies or elevators, or me.

My mother is a believer in absolutes. She believes there is a right time and place for things. If I ask her "When *is* someday?" she always says, "When it is the absolutely right time for you to know a thing. Then you will know. Absolutely." Like the time when I was a little younger, when we were standing in a crowded elevator and I decided that would be a good moment to ask her a pressing question.

"What's a period?" I asked. To be honest, I pretty much already knew because in Phys. Ed. class we'd seen a movie about girls becoming women. So I guess I was just testing her to see how *she* would explain it to me.

"It's a thing that comes at the end of a sentence," she said without looking at me. I noticed people were grinning.

"What else?"

"What 'what else?' That's it. It's a mark to end a sentence. It's a punctuation mark. That's it."

"But what *else* is it?"

"Nothing else."

"Yes, it is. It's something else. I know it is." I remember feeling a little upset, as if I were beginning to convince myself that I didn't know the other meaning after all.

"Then I don't know."

"Yes, you do." By now everyone else was either smiling quietly up at the ceiling or down at their shoes.

"Then maybe it's some English word I don't know." She still wasn't really looking at me.

We got off the elevator, leaving people curious about how it was all going to end. And of course, walking down the hall, my mother said "Someday you'll understand."

"Yeah," I said, teasing her, "Just like someday you'll understand who Neil Diamond is, and what Madeleine books are, and about barbecues, and how to make tacos, and you'll know all the words to the Christmas carols." These are the things my mother cannot help me with since she didn't grow up with the music most of my friends' parents did, or learn the same songs, or eat fast food. She also can't help me with math—except for, luckily, the metric system, which she *did* grow up with and which all my teachers say will soon be used on milk cartons and soda bottles and everything everywhere. I always check when we go to the supermarket, but so far there's no sign of this big change. They can take their time, though, because I just started to understand ounces, pounds, inches, and feet. But my mother tells me math is a beautiful thing because it's based on principles, which is another word for absolutes. She says I should try to love it for that, even though it's difficult. "Like some people?" I ask her, hinting.

My French homework is another thing she can't help me with. She says it sounds like Greek to her. Fortunately, I don't need her help with French anyway. I always get *A*'s on my exams and my pronunciation is very good. My teacher says I have an ear. My mother isn't surprised. She's always happy when I do well, but she's never surprised. She thinks that between her and my father, whom I don't remember very well because he died when I was a baby, I should have an ear for languages. His parents were from Germany, and even though they moved to America when he was very little, he listened to them talking all the time and so he had a very good accent. It was so good in fact that my mother says he fooled her into thinking he knew a lot more German than he really did. He grew up in New York and my mother met him when she came to the States a few years after World War II. He'd been a soldier with the U.S. Army during the war. He was even awarded the Purple Heart, which is a medal given for bravery by the U.S. military. He had a mustache and my mother says he would comb it a certain way and do this ridiculous imitation of Hitler. She says that after such an evil man as Hitler and experiencing so much loss and cruelty in the war, sometimes they had to make jokes or they might've gone crazy.

People say I have my father's smile. Sometimes, usually when my grandmother visits, my mother reaches out and pulls a strand of my long brown hair across the space over my mouth as if it were a mustache like my father's. Then they laugh their heads off at the family resemblance, amazed, teary laughs. And they start to speak Polish to each other, very fast, faster than when they talk on the telephone. Sometimes I pull the hair over my mouth myself, just to make my mother laugh. Sometimes I wish we had to learn Polish in school instead of French, just so I could understand what they're talking about.

Anyway, if I did need help with French, I could always ask my sort-of friend Ginny who speaks French fluently because she lived in Switzerland with her mother for a few years. After Ginny's parents got divorced her mother got a job teaching English to Swiss kids. They also travelled a lot together. Ginny wears her blonde hair in two braids pinned up across the top of her head like a little crown—just like the Madame Alexandra doll I have, or the Pennsylvania Dutch Noodle and Swiss Miss Hot Cocoa girls in the TV commercials. Maybe she's only my sort-of friend because I'm a bit jealous of her, and she's a bit conceited. I don't know too many people who've been many places, except for my mother who's been to Czechoslavakia and Poland. But the Eastern bloc is not all that fascinating to me. I'd rather hear about real places, like Paris and Hawaii. I thought Ginny would be willing to tell me. But she turned out to be worse than my mother was when I asked her about periods. For example, "What's different about Paris?" I asked her.

"Nothing."

"Well, there must be something."

"I don't know. Nothing really."

"Well, what about Italy?"

"I don't know! Questions, questions!" she'd say, climbing around the matched set of imported furniture in her pink palace bedroom.

I couldn't believe her. Even where my grandmother lives in Arizona is different from my green little New England town. Places that are even further away must be even more different—different trees, smells, clothes. Ginny made me feel ashamed of being curious, and I didn't feel like spending too much time with her after that. Her house isn't that much fun anyway. You can't sit on her bed, much less jump, because the "puff" might come out of her comforter. And her comforter is covered with a hundred little sewed-on bows just begging to be untied.

Still, my mother reminds me that even China and the United States made some kind of peace in the years since I'd started school. Maybe there's hope for Ginny and me yet. I do have to admit, Ginny has good taste. We played hide-and-seek once when I slept over and I hid in her closet just so I could look at all her clothes. I kept thinking about how a lot of them had come from different countries around the world. She even had shoes with high heels on them and a little fur jacket. Very grownup.

When my mother picked me up the next morning, Ginny stood waving to us from her front porch. She was wearing her silky pink "morning robe" that has a big pink feathery kind of collar that her mother called a "boa," and she was wearing these pink slippers with skinny little heels and fluffy pom-poms on the toes. Her mother called them "mules." I liked those slippers. I wanted some exactly like them.

"Ginny has very sophisticated-looking clothes," my mother said as we pulled out of the driveway. I told her about the little fur jacket and the shoes too, even though I didn't like the jacket as much because it was rabbit and I didn't like to think what that meant.

"Very grownup," she said. "I wonder what she will have left to look forward to when she really does grow up." She started to tell me it wasn't good to get certain things too soon because it takes the fun out of having them.

"Variety is the spice of life," she said. She likes that saying, she says it a lot. "Why have everything at once?" She said there were all kinds of things—like driving a car and travelling, and high heels and even romance—that, to be really enjoyed, were better saved for their proper time and place. She had me pretty convinced. After all, I don't like to open birthday or Christmas presents early, as some of my friends do. I would hate to be so impatient that there would be nothing left to open on those days. But I'd still like a pair of those mules.

On the way home from Ginny's that day, my mother makes a detour. She drives past a little stone cottage and through an iron gate into a private section of town called Knotty Woods.

"Wealthy Woods is what they should call it," my grandmother says. She thinks it's a waste for my mother to make the sacrifices she makes to live "above her means" in an expensive town like ours.

My mother says she and my grandmother have different priorities. She says we'll live wherever we like.

Usually there is a guard sitting in the cottage, but this time he isn't there. We drive along the winding, twisting roads of Knotty Woods. It is even more crowded with trees than the regular parts of town, and sometimes you have to look very closely to see the big houses hidden in all the greenery. Some are made of gray stone and blend in with the paths and brooks that dot the woods surrounding them. Others are much lighter colored, with dark wood beams outlining the roofs and windows. They all look full of nooks and crannies. My mother drives into a small clearing and parks the car. We've driven around here before, once to drop off one of my classmates from school. But we've never actually gotten out of the car and walked in the woods.

"Are you sure it's all right?" I ask as she motions me to come out with her.

"Nonsense," she says. "Don't be silly."

We walk for a little while in the woods behind the houses. It's very quiet and a little dark because the tree branches meet over our heads and cover up the sky. My mother starts collecting fallen chestnuts, holding them in the front of her blouse which she has pulled out of her skirt. After she's gathered enough we sit on the cool ground and she takes off her shoes. She looks to me like a really young girl, sitting on the ground with her new toys, wiggling her toes. Suddenly I can imagine her other life, riding horses, gathering freshly laid eggs.

"I've waited a long time for this," she says. She reaches out and rolls a couple of crab apples toward us. When I see her smiling and her cheeks flushing, I think that maybe some things are worth waiting for. I think maybe I begin to understand.

# ONE LAST TIME

## Gary Soto

GARY SOTO was born in Fresno, California and grew up in and around the fields of the San Joaquin Valley, the subject of his autobiographical collections *Small Faces*, *Living Up the Street*, and *A Summer Life*. Soto graduated magna cum laude from California State University at Fresno. He has written poetry and fiction for adults and young people, and has produced three short films, including the award-winning *The Pool Party*. He lives in Berkeley, California.

Yesterday I saw the movie *Gandhi* and recognized a few of the people—not in the theater but in the film. I saw my relatives, dusty and thin as sparrows, returning from the fields with hoes balanced on their shoulders. The workers were squinting, eyes small and veined, and were using their hands to say what there was to say to those in the audience with popcorn and Cokes. I didn't have anything, though. I sat thinking of my family and their years in the fields, beginning with Grandmother who came to the United States after the Mexican revolution to settle in Fresno where she met her husband and bore children, many of them. She worked in the fields around Fresno, picking grapes, oranges, plums, peaches, and cotton, dragging a large white sack like a sled. She worked in the packing houses, Bonner and

Sun-Maid Raisin, where she stood at a conveyor belt passing her hand over streams of raisins to pluck out leaves and pebbles. For over twenty years she worked at a machine that boxed raisins until she retired at sixty-five.

Grandfather worked in the fields, as did his children. Mother also found herself out there when she separated from Father for three weeks. I remember her coming home, dusty and so tired that she had to rest on the porch before she trudged inside to wash and start dinner. I didn't understand the complaints about her ankles or the small of her back, even though I had been in the grape fields watching her work. With my brother and sister I ran in and out of the rows; we enjoyed ourselves and pretended not to hear Mother scolding us to sit down and behave ourselves. A few years later, however, I caught on when I went to pick grapes rather than play in the rows.

Mother and I got up before dawn and ate quick bowls of cereal. She drove in silence while I rambled on how everything was now solved, how I was going to make enough money to end our misery and even buy her a beautiful copper teapot, the one I had shown her in Long's Drugs. When we arrived I was frisky and ready to go, self-consciously aware of my grape knife dangling at my wrist. I almost ran to the row the foreman had pointed out, but I returned to help Mother with the grape pans and jug of water. She told me to settle down and reminded me not to lose my knife. I walked at her side and listened to her explain how to cut grapes; bent down, hands on knees, I watched her demonstrate by cutting a few bunches into my pan. She stood over me as I tried it myself, tugging at a bunch of grapes that pulled loose like beads from a necklace. "Cut the stem all the way," she told me as last advice before she walked away, her shoes sinking in the loose dirt, to begin work on her own row.

I cut another bunch, then another, fighting the snap and whip of vines. After ten minutes of groping for grapes, my first pan brimmed with bunches. I poured them on the paper tray, which was bordered by a wooden frame that kept the grapes from rolling off, and they spilled like jewels from a pirate's chest. The tray was only half filled, so I hurried to jump under the vines and begin groping, cutting, and tugging at the grapes again. I emptied the pan, raked the grapes with my hands to make them look like they filled the tray, and jumped back under the vine on my knees. I tried to cut faster because Mother, in the next row, was slowly moving ahead. I peeked into her row and saw five trays gleaming in the early morning. I cut, pulled hard, and stopped to gather the grapes that missed the pan; already bored, I spat on a few to wash them before tossing them like popcorn into my mouth.

So it went. Two pans equaled one tray—or six cents. By lunchtime I had a trail of thirty-seven trays behind me while Mother had sixty or more. We met about halfway from our last trays, and I sat down with a grunt, knees wet from kneeling on dropped grapes. I washed my hands with the water from the jug, drying them on the inside of my shirt sleeve before I opened the paper bag for the first sandwich, which I gave to Mother. I dipped my hand in again to unwrap a sandwich without looking at it. I took a first bite and chewed it slowly for the tang of mustard. Eating in silence I looked straight ahead at the vines, and only when we were finished with cookies did we talk.

"Are you tired?" she asked.

"No, but I got a sliver from the frame," I told her. I showed her the web of skin between my thumb and index finger. She wrinkled her forehead but said it was nothing.

"How many trays did you do?"

I looked straight ahead, not answering at first. I recounted in my mind the whole morning of bend, cut, pour again and again, before answering a feeble "Thirty-seven." No elaboration, no detail. Without looking at me she told me how she had done field work in Texas and Michigan as a child. But I had a difficult time listening to her stories. I played with my grape knife, stabbing it into the ground, but stopped when Mother reminded me that I had better not lose it. I left the knife sticking up like a small, leafless plant. She then talked about school, the junior high I would be going to that fall, and then about Rick and Debra, how sorry they would be that they hadn't come out to pick grapes because they'd have no new clothes for the school year.

She stopped talking when she peeked at her watch, a bandless one she kept in her pocket. She got up with an "*Ay, Dios,*" and told me that we'd work until three, leaving me cutting figures in the sand with my knife and dreading the return to work.

Finally I rose and walked slowly back to where I had left off, again kneeling under the vine and fixing the pan under bunches of grapes. By that time, 11:30, the sun was over my shoulder and made me squint and think of the pool at the YMCA where I was a summer member. I saw myself diving face-first into the water and loving it. I saw myself gleaming like something new, at the edge of the pool. I had to daydream and keep my mind busy because boredom was a terror almost as awful as the work itself. My mind went dumb with stupid things, and I had to keep it moving with dreams of baseball and would-be girlfriends. I even sang, however softly, to keep my mind moving, my hands moving.

I worked less hurriedly and with less vision. I no longer saw that copper pot sitting squat on our stove or Mother waiting for it to whistle. The wardrobe that I imagined, crisp and bright in the closet, numbered only one pair of jeans and two shirts because, in half a day, six cents times thirty-seven trays was two dollars and twenty-two cents. It became clear to me. If I worked eight hours, I might make four dollars. I'd take this, even gladly, and walk downtown to look into store windows on the mall and long for the bright madras shirts from Walter Smith or Coffee's, but settling for two imitation ones from Penney's.

That first day I laid down seventy-three trays while Mother had a hundred and twenty behind her. On the back of an old envelope, she wrote out our numbers and hours. We washed at the pump behind the farm house and walked slowly to our car for the drive back to town in the afternoon heat. That evening after dinner I sat in a lawn chair listening to music from a transistor radio while Rick and David King played catch. I joined them in a game of pickle, but there was little joy in trying to avoid their tags because I couldn't get the fields out of my mind: I saw myself dropping on my knees under a vine to tug at a branch that wouldn't come off. In bed, when I closed my eyes, I saw the fields, yellow with kicked-up dust, and a crooked trail of trays rotting behind me.

The next day I woke tired and started picking tired. The grapes rained into the pan, slowly filling like a belly, until I had my first tray and started my second. So it went all day, and the next, and all through the following week, so that by the end of thirteen days the foreman counted out, in tens mostly, my pay of fifty-three dollars. Mother earned one hundred and forty-eight dollars. She wrote this on her envelope, with a message I didn't bother to ask her about.

The next day I walked with my friend Scott to the downtown mall where we drooled over the clothes behind fancy windows, bought popcorn, and sat at a tier of outdoor fountains to talk about girls. Finally we went into Penney's for more popcorn, which we ate walking around, before we returned home without buying anything. It wasn't until a few days before school that I let my fifty-three dollars slip quietly from my hands, buying a pair of pants, two shirts, and a maroon T-shirt, the kind that was in style. At home I tried them on while Rick looked on enviously; later, the day before school started, I tried them on again wondering not so much if they were worth it as who would see me first in those clothes.

Along with my brother and sister I picked grapes until I was fifteen, before giving up and saying that I'd rather wear old clothes than stoop like a Mexican. Mother thought I was being stuck-up, even stupid, because there would be no clothes for me in the fall. I told her I didn't care, but when Rick and Debra rose at five in the morning, I lay awake in bed feeling that perhaps I had made a mistake but unwilling to change my mind. That fall Mother bought me two pairs of socks, a packet of colored T-shirts, and underwear. The T-shirts would help, I thought, but who would see that I had new underwear and socks? I wore a new T-shirt on the first day of school, then an old shirt on Tuesday, than another T-shirt on Wednesday, and on Thursday an old Nehru shirt that was embarrassingly out of style. On Friday I changed into the corduroy pants my brother had handed down to me and slipped into my last new T-shirt. I worked like a magician, blinding my classmates, who were all clothes-conscious and small-time social climbers, by arranging my wardrobe to make it seem larger than it really was. But by spring I had to do something—my blue jeans were almost silver and my shoes had lost their form, puddling like black ice around my feet. That spring of my sixteenth year, Rick and I decided to take a labor bus to chop cotton. In his old Volkswagen, which was more noise than power, we drove on a Saturday morning to West Fresno—or Chinatown, as some call it—parked, walked slowly toward a bus, and stood gawking at the winos, toothy blacks, Okies, *Tejanos* with gold teeth, whores, Mexican families, and labor contractors shouting "Cotton" or "Beets," the work of spring.

We boarded the "Cotton" bus without looking at the contractor who stood almost blocking the entrance because he didn't want winos. We boarded scared and then were more scared because two blacks in the rear were drunk and arguing loudly about what was better, a two-barrel or four-barrel Ford carburetor. We sat far from them, looking straight ahead, and only glanced briefly at the others who boarded, almost all of them broken and poorly dressed in loudly mismatched clothes. Finally when the contractor banged his palm against the side of the bus, the young man at the wheel, smiling and talking in Spanish, started the engine, idled it for a moment while he adjusted the mirrors, and started off in slow chugs. Except for the windshield there was no glass in the windows, so as soon as we were on the rural roads outside Fresno, the dust and sand began to be sucked into the bus, whipping about like irate wasps as the gravel ticked about us. We closed our eyes, clotted up our mouths that wanted to open with embarrassed laughter because we couldn't believe we were on that bus with those people and the dust attacking us for no reason.

When we arrived at a field we followed the others to a pickup where we each took a hoe and marched to stand before a row. Rick and I, self-conscious and unsure, looked around at the others who leaned on their hoes or squatted in front of the rows, almost all talking in Spanish, joking, lighting cigarettes—

all waiting for the foreman's whistle to begin work. Mother had explained how to chop cotton by showing us with a broom in the backyard.

"Like this," she said, her broom swishing down weeds. "Leave one plant and cut four—and cut them! Don't leave them standing or the foreman will get mad."

The foreman whistled and we started up the row, stealing glances at other workers to see if we were doing it right. But after a while we worked like we knew what we were doing, neither of us hurrying or falling behind. But slowly the clot of men, women, and kids began to spread and loosen. Even Rick pulled away. I didn't hurry, though. I cut smoothly and cleanly as I walked at a slow pace, in a sort of funeral march. My eyes measured each space of cotton plants before I cut. If I missed the plants, I swished again. I worked intently, seldom looking up, so when I did I was amazed to see the sun, like a broken orange coin, in the east. It looked blurry, unbelievable, like something not of this world. I looked around in amazement, scanning the eastern horizon that was a taut line jutted with an occasional mountain. The horizon was beautiful, like a snapshot of the moon, in the early light of morning, in the quiet of no cars and few people.

The foreman trudged in boots in my direction, stepping awkwardly over the plants, to inspect the work. No one around me looked up. We all worked steadily while we waited for him to leave. When he did leave, with a feeble complaint addressed to no one in particular, we looked up smiling under straw hats and bandanas.

By 11:00, our lunch time, my ankles were hurting from walking on clods the size of hardballs. My arms ached and my face was dusted by a wind that was perpetual, always busy whipping about. But the work was not bad, I thought. It was better, so much better, than picking grapes, especially with the hourly wage of a dollar twenty-five instead of piece work. Rick and I walked sorely toward the bus where we washed and drank water. Instead of eating in the bus or in the shade of the bus, we kept to ourselves by walking down to the irrigation canal that ran the length of the field, to open our lunch of sandwiches and crackers. We laughed at the crackers, which seemed like a cruel joke from our mother, because we were working under the sun and the last thing we wanted was a salty dessert. We ate them anyway and drank more water before we returned to the field, both of us limping in exaggeration. Working side by side, we talked and laughed at our predicament because our Mother had warned us year after year that if we didn't get on track in school we'd have to work in the fields and then we would see. We mimicked Mother's whining voice and smirked at her smoky view of the future in which we'd be trapped by marriage and screaming kids. We'd eat beans and then we'd see.

Rick pulled slowly away to the rhythm of his hoe falling faster and smoother. It was better that way, to work alone. I could hum made-up songs or songs from the radio and think to myself about school and friends. At the time I was doing badly in my classes, mainly because of a difficult stepfather, but also because I didn't care anymore. All through junior high and into my first year of high school there were those who said I would never do anything, be anyone. They said I'd work like a donkey and marry the first Mexican girl that came along. I was reminded so often, verbally and in the way I was treated at home, that I began to believe that chopping cotton might be a lifetime job for me. If not chopping cotton, then I might get lucky and find myself in a car wash or restaurant or junkyard. But it was clear; I'd work, and work hard.

I cleared my mind by humming and looking about. The sun was directly above with a few soft blades of clouds against a sky that seemed bluer and more beautiful than our sky in the city. Occasionally the breeze flurried and picked up dust so that I had to cover my eyes and screw up my face. The workers were hunched, brown as the clods under our feet, and spread across the field that ran without end—fields that were owned by corporations, not families.

I hoed trying to keep my mind busy with scenes from school and pretend girlfriends until finally my brain turned off and my thinking went fuzzy with boredom. I looked about, no longer mesmerized by the beauty of the landscape, no longer wondering if the winos in the fields could hold out for eight hours, no longer dreaming of the clothes I'd buy with my pay. My eyes followed my chopping as the plants, thin as their shadows, fell with each strike. I worked slowly with ankles and arms hurting, neck stiff, and eyes stinging from the dust and the sun that glanced off the field like a mirror.

By quitting time, 3:00, there was such an excruciating pain in my ankles that I walked as if I were wearing snowshoes. Rick laughed at me and I laughed too, embarrassed that most of the men were walking normally and I was among the first timers who had to get used to this work. "And what about you, wino," I came back at Rick. His eyes were meshed red and his long hippie hair was flecked with dust and gnats and bits of leaves. We placed our hoes in the back of a pickup and stood in line for our pay, which was twelve-fifty. I was amazed at the pay, which was the most I had ever earned in one day, and thought that I'd come back the next day, Sunday. This was too good.

Instead of joining the others in the labor bus, we jumped in the back of a pickup when the driver said we'd get to town sooner and were welcome to join him. We scrambled into the truck bed to be joined by a heavy-set and laughing *Tejano* whose head was shaped like an egg, particularly so because the bandana he wore ended in a point on the top of his head. He laughed almost demonically as the pickup roared up the dirt path, a gray cape of dust rising behind us. On the highway, with the wind in our faces, we squinted at the fields as if we were looking for someone. The *Tejano* had quit laughing but was smiling broadly, occasionally chortling tunes he never finished. I was scared of him, though Rick, two years older and five inches taller, wasn't. If the *Tejano* looked at him, Rick stared back for a second or two before he looked away to the fields.

I felt like a soldier coming home from war when we rattled into Chinatown. People leaning against car hoods stared, their necks following us, owl-like; prostitutes chewed gum more ferociously and showed us their teeth; Chinese grocers stopped brooming their storefronts to raise their cadaverous faces at us.

We stopped in front of the Chi Chi Club where Mexican music blared from the juke box and cue balls cracked like dull ice. The *Tejano*, who was dirty as we were, stepped awkwardly over the side rail, dusted himself off with his bandana, and sauntered into the club.

Rick and I jumped from the back, thanked the driver who said *de nada* and popped his clutch, so that the pickup jerked and coughed blue smoke. We returned smiling to our car, happy with the money we had made and pleased that we had, in a small way, proved ourselves to be tough; that we worked as well as other men and earned the same pay.

We returned the next day and the next week until the season was over and there was nothing to do. I told myself that I wouldn't pick grapes that summer, saying all through June and July that it was for Mexicans, not me. When August came around and I still had not found a summer job, I ate my words, sharpened my knife, and joined Mother, Rick, and Debra for one last time.

## Hisaye Yamamoto

HISAYE YAMAMOTO was born in Redondo Beach, California, and was one of the first Japanese American writers to gain recognition after the Second World War. She has been writing for publication since the age of fourteen, first for Japanese American newspapers, and then, during the war, for the newspaper in the internment camp where she and her family were held. After the war, she wrote for newspapers and literary magazines. In 1986 she received a lifetime achievement award from the Before Columbus Foundation. A collection of stories, *Seventeen Syllables and Other Stories*, was published in 1988.

"The Enormous Piano" describes her memories of growing up in California before the war.

> *In truth I seem to have felt mostly the joys of living, in remembering, in recording . . . it is the pain.*
>
> —ROBERT LOWELL

There are some who can literally go home again, who can travel back to certain villages and towns and point out the very house in which they were born.

I don't think there are many Nisei who can do this. There were two important barriers to our rooting anywhere: the withholding of citizenship to our parents and the prohibition against their purchasing property. While California welcomed both Chinese and Japanese as long as they remained laborers, the state became alarmed about the Yellow Peril and enacted laws prohibiting both citizenship and property-owning for Asians. The Chinese Exclusion Act of 1882 and the Asian Exclusion Act of 1942 were not to be lifted until the Second World War for the Chinese and 1952 for the Japanese, as part of the McCarran-Walter Act.

Although I did not know it at the time, these were the reasons why our family seemed to be forever moving. As soon as the lease on the land was up, off we would go to farm another promising spot.

Before I was twenty, there were, I think, four moves in the Redondo Beach area, Downey, Artesia, Norwalk, Hynes (then known as the Greatest Hay and Dairy Center in the World and now known as Paramount), and Oceanside. So aside from our relatives and our parents' Old Country contacts, permanent connections were few.

When I try to remember, I look for a plain little girl whose hair was chopped straight across her forehead and who spoke only Japanese.

Of my earliest days, I know nothing. My past is hidden in swirling mists, in which I can almost but not quite make out the dim shapes of people, places, events, mostly from hearsay.

When I was old enough to wonder, I would ask my parents where I had been born. They were sure it was a place called, as closely as I could make out, Peh-ri.

Later, as I learned English, I decided it must be Perry, but could find no such place on the map.

Finally, in 1942, on the eve of evacuation, when it seemed important to ascertain the place of my birth (my brothers all had birth certificates but not I), I sent to the county recorder and found out I had been born in Redondo Beach. Not that finding out I was American-born made any difference. Our family, along with some one hundred ten thousand Japanese, in what was called the Western Defense Command, were uprooted and shipped to inland concentration camps for most of the duration of the War.

Why Peh-ri? The only thing I can figure is that there is a Perry Avenue thereabouts, and maybe that was where my folks were living at the time.

I recall my mother saying that she once walked carrying me to catch the Red Car, but that I fell asleep in her arms, so she bedded me down in some tall weeds en route and picked me up on her way home.

There was an American family across the street that had a daughter named Carrie who doted on me, or so I was told. It was Carrie's mother who had tutored my mother in English when she first arrived from Japan. And it was in those first years that I was kicked in the head by a horse.

My father said he was guiding the horse-drawn cultivator between two tall rows of Kentucky beans, when the horse abruptly stopped and refused to budge. Then my father spied me, my head bleeding where the horse's hoof had struck, sitting in the bean row under the horse.

I can hear the triumphant cries, "Aha, that explains everything!" But it doesn't really. A few years later, I was playing on the front seat of the car and, falling over backwards, managed to poke a hole in my head with the choke.

My mother was giving an order to the deliveryman from the Kameya Grocery in Moneta, and the man said, "Your daughter's crying." My mother kept on with the ordering—five-gallon wooden vats of bean paste and soy sauce, a hundred pounds of rice—and said "Oh, she's always crying."

I clearly remember those words and lying in bed for days afterwards with my entire head wrapped in bandages. I remember because that second accident occurred much later, two moves after my birthplace, which we left for a hilly dirt road lined with towering eucalyptus.

There seemed to be other Japanese farm families living along the road. Two of my brothers, Johnny and Jemo, must have been born there, but I recall only three happenings, all of them unhappy.

My mother made me a dress of flannel and the other children hooted to see me wearing it, saying that I was wearing nightclothes. She made a lot of those, too, on her treadle Singer, with self-belts to secure the *nemaki* around us.

Another day, playing house with several other children

down the road, I was persuaded to eat one of the concoctions of mud, because (I was told) all the other kids had, and besides, if I didn't I wouldn't be allowed in the game. I can feel the grit between my teeth to this day.

The last incident is apocryphal: I was with two or three other children, bigger, and for some reason they helped me to climb a roadside apple tree. They left and I remained in the tree until dusk, afraid to jump, until my father came along in the car, looking for me.

The mists begin to evaporate by our third move. But I recall no wind or rain or fog, only a succession of sun-filled days under clear blue skies. The rest is somewhat like a thousand-piece jigsaw puzzle, in which I can fit together some rather large sections, but then there are these gaping holes here and there.

When we moved, we took our dog along in a gunny sack. It was a collie that had been given to us by a couple who had returned to Japan. I don't remember the man and woman but they left a photograph of themselves in which he, small, is seated, and she, large, stands beside him. She has strong eyebrows and a wide-brimmed straw hat. I believe the dog died around moving day, and there was mention of him having eaten poison.

En route to our new place, we stopped near an oil derrick. It had the usual sump hole, a rectangular reservoir of thick black goo. My grandfather climbed the earthen embankment and dropped the gunny sack in.

Our new home, a green clapboard with white window frames, was a long one, with the kitchen-dining room on one end (my mother emptied a sack of rice into the pull-out flour bin) and the bedroom on the far end.

In the middle was the living room, opening onto a wide front platform, and this was the room that contained the enormous piano. The piano belonged to our landlord. It was black and had a hinged bench to match. It took up a whole corner and was bigger than the bed in the diagonal corner where my grandfather slept.

Grandpa Yamamoto was planning to go back to Japan,

his fortune made, to join his wife and two other children. It had been taken for granted that he would take me with him when he went so that I could have a proper Japanese upbringing.

There was a huge family orchard alongside the long sandy road from the street to the house. There were peaches, apples, apricots, pears, plums. My brothers and I played there or in the irrigation ditches, catching the little doodlebugs that squiggled down backwards to make cone-shaped traps for their quarry.

We went looking for burnt matches to bundle with rubber bands and bury as treasure. We sat on the supports of wooden flumes, our feet in the flowing water, telling stories about the drips and blobs that had spilled from the sealing tar and formed silhouettes of a camel, a tree, a flower, a face. We didn't get much candy, but we chewed hardened tar and snacked on tidbits that were more salt or sour than sweet: pickled scallions, tiny dried fish, the tough and salty leaves of dried seaweed, and we used to tear off strips of dried cuttlefish to chew until they were shreds tender enough to swallow.

Another brother, Yuke, was born. I was the oldest, so I still wandered about by myself, east, west, south, but I don't remember going very far north.

North of the house were the outbuildings, the bathhouse, the *benjo*, the stable where the horse was kept and the barn where my mother buried jars of *koru-mame* to stickily ripen between bales of hay.

In the barn I once found a box containing a pair of high-button shoes and a stiff hat of reddish-brown crinkled velvet with a spray of black feathers.

My mother had worn accessories such as these in the photographs in the trunk, but her usual attire was whipcord breeches, shirt, white poke bonnet and long homemade gloves of cotton print which left the fingers free to pick strawberries and such.

In the front yard, next to the porch, my mother grew slender ferny cosmos of pink, lavender, white; everlasting strawflowers with tiny purple blossoms; and dahlias.

Crime abounded. My grandfather axe-murdered a chicken for dinner and the headless bird kept running around frantically for a while before it dropped. My father came home hush-hush from the beach with illegal abalone hidden under the hood of the old black Ford. We ate it raw, thinly sliced, with a sauce of *shoyu* and vinegar.

My mother made *sake* and hid it in the bedroom closet. One New Year's, at my aunt's, there was a rumor that revenuers had been spotted in the neighborhood, so everyone dumped his *sake* into the sink, hastily rinsed the smell of mulled *sake* out of the little decanters and cups, and we all sat around pretending to be innocent partakers of a New Year's feast. But it turned out later to have been a false alarm. All this subterfuge was necessary because Prohibition had been the law of the land since 1919. So our status as bootleggers lasted until 1933 when it became legal to make and drink "intoxicating liquors" again.

On another New Year's Eve, a trio of young Italians, two men and a woman, who lived nearby, came plunging into our kitchen with accordion, song, and laughter. We looked up startled from the table, where we may have been having our *soba* and *tororo*. There is frozen in my memory still the picture of that lovely young woman as she entered the screen door, her hair dark and long, and her teeth white and laughing.

Somewhere along here, there was a funeral. It was a newborn baby of friends who had come from the same village as my parents. They had a couple of children already, a boy named Toshi and a girl named Chiyoto, both older than I. There was only a graveside service, for which we all stood scattered around on a rather barren hillside which was either the entire cemetery or a far corner of it.

There was a German family across the way to the east, name of Miller (Mueller?), with a son named Tony. The mother was ample, with short straight blonde hair. She spoke English with an accent, I suppose, but in those days German and English were all the same to me. Her apple pies seemed to have a thin soap-textured layer just before the bottom crust, so I approached the layer gingerly, wondering if eating the soap was worth the delight of sweetened apples.

The father was swarthy, mustached, and also spoke oddly. In his closed garage, with trousers rolled up and feet bare, he would climb into a barrel and smash grapes. I could tell he didn't like me coming around. Neither did his son Tony, who always wore a beanie.

Later when I began kindergarten, my mother asked Tony to look after me the first day. He agreed, but at school he pretended as though he didn't know me from Adam.

Past the Millers to the east there was a Japanese family with several children. They had a kitchen garden in which purple *shiso* grew. When the children were bad, the mother burnt little black squares of incense on their backs.

One day I ran onto the Millers' porch and their collie, startled from sleep, jumped up and sank his teeth into my knee. It was their Japanese neighbor, the father of my friends, who carried me to my home on his back. I was taken to the doctor, who took a burning hot spoon, shaped like a muddle, and cooked the wounds in my knee until they closed.

Was it fear then that prompted my first lies?

Usually I was sent after the mail, which the postman in his auto dropped off at several mailboxes lined up together at a corner some distance away.

Once when I went after the mail, a white girl came out from the chicken farm across the street and asked me questions. She had a paper from which she asked the questions and a pencil to write my answers down.

I didn't understand a word she was saying, but I judiciously nodded or shook my head and answered yes or no whenever she came to a stop. Years later, it occurred to me that maybe it hadn't been a true-or-false questionnaire at all, but at the time I had a sense of having handled the situation magnificently.

After the dogbite, I feared dogs. Once when my mother asked me to go after the mail, I remembered the white poodle at the chicken farm. I went partway and clamped my teeth down on my arm deeply enough to make indentations, then returned home. I told my mother that I couldn't possibly go after the mail because a dog had bitten me, and I showed her the teethmarks as proof.

Another time, she asked me to go and tell my father that lunch was ready. He was working in our farthest field, beyond the Miller house. I went as far as the irrigation well and bounced up and down for a while on the heavy and weathered loose planks that covered the well. Then I went home and my mother asked if I had summoned my father. I assured her I had.

On the hill in the other direction, westward, was a Japanese family who lived in a big house. Their yard contained a pomegranate tree and a large rectangular concrete fishpond with goldfish darting to and fro or resting under water lily pads. Sometimes I was allowed to break up some little round slices of pinkish dried bread to feed the fish. The bits of bread expanded in the water and floated until an open mouth darted up to gulp.

Past the chicken farm was another Japanese family called Miura. They seemed to be prosperous. There were a boy and a girl, both older, who tolerated me.

Once the girl took me along on a walk and we wandered into an unused chicken yard. She wore long white cotton stockings and she walked around letting fleas land on them. Then we went to sit on a stoop nearby, and it was a revelation watching her squish one dark flea after another between her thumbnails. She smashed with relish, and I envied her the long white stockings which made such a project possible.

But my best friend was Sadae-san, lately returned from Japan, who was engaged to be married. Once she gave me a hot sweet soup made of Indian beans, but she wouldn't let me eat it immediately. She kept asking me if there wasn't something I should say first.

She was ironing as I guessed and guessed. I stared hungrily at the little white shapes of flower and leaf afloat on the soup, but Sadae-san kept ironing and shaking her head inexorably, no, I couldn't eat just yet. Finally, after ignorance had almost lost me my appetite, she told me what I was supposed to say: "Thank you." It was English she had wanted, English I never in my life would have thought of. So I echoed it with great relief and set to sipping the sweet, dark, thick soup at last.

When Sadae-san was married, I was one of the flower girls.

Her family took me to Los Angeles to have my hair marcelled for the occasion and buy me a white dress. The other flower girl, older, was from San Pedro. She was lovely, with full lips. Her white dress was fancier. My mother said privately that she had wanted to buy my dress, but no, they had insisted and now look.

Before the wedding, Sadae-san took me on the Red Car to the pier at Redondo Beach. She treated me to a cowboy movie, but the shooting frightened me and, wanting desperately to get away, I told her I had seen it before. She laughed and called me a liar.

She also wanted me to ride on the merry-go-round, but I balked. I was willing to settle for a safe seat on the gilt chariot, but the attendant would not permit it.

Grandpa Yamamoto also took me to Redondo Beach before he sailed back to Japan. He took me by the hand and we walked over interminable hills sprouting everywhere with oil derricks.

The only other memory I have of him is a rear view of his wielding a shovel on the outskirts of the field nearest the house. Wearing workclothes and his chauffeur's cap, he was damming up the rows that filled with water and opening up adjacent dry rows. I wondered, too, about a story that was told of him, of his having been on a bicycle and in a collision with an automobile at a country intersection. The story was that he had been split up the rear.

Of his day of departure, I have no memory. There must have been luggage, presents for the homefolk, and a huge ship such as I later remember taking others to Japan.

There would have been the same festive air, produced in part by the man on board banging a baton on a large metal pan to let us know it was time to get off, but mainly by the streamers of multicolored paper flying to and from the ship and pier until the entangled serpentine was a thick solid rainbow mass that grew wider and wider as the ship moved away. Bit by bit, the connection tore asunder, to float on the water and strew the pier. It was a joy to be able to retrieve a partial roll or two for later, to play with at home.

For some reason, I did not go to Japan with my grandfather. Was it then my nightmares ended?

It was the same dream every time: there I was in the middle of the Pacific Ocean, which fortunately seemed to be only waist-high. But I sensed that it could immediately roil deeper in either direction and engulf me at any time. I could not for the life of me make up my mind whether to wade on towards Japan or try and make it back to California. Always I would wake up terrified of drowning, anguished by my indecision.

But as I have indicated, the chronology of these remembrances is suspect. It may very well have been that the nightmares did not end with my grandfather's leaving. Perhaps that was when they began.

As for the enormous piano—ah, yes, the piano. We must have banged on it as children will. And it may have been that, plucking on the keys with her index finger, my mother sang a school song that seemed to make her happy and sad at the same time. I think this began, *Kon-go seki wo mina kazuba*, and I can hum the next line, but I forget the rest.

One day Mrs. Noda came to call. She had come from the same Japanese village about the same time as my mother, and she had a son, Seichi, the same year I was born. I was sitting backwards on the piano bench and, made shy by company, I began banging the back of my head on the keys.

"Look, look, look what she's doing!" Mrs. Noda said to my mother, and my mother reproached me.

The way I figure it, that piano was at least eight feet across, with at least three-foot-wide sides, and about five feet high. I have never come across another like it.

Naomi Shihab Nye

When NAOMI SHIHAB NYE was fourteen, her family moved from Missouri to Jerusalem (then divided between Jordan and Israel) to live near her Arab relatives for a year, the subject of "Thank You in Arabic." She now lives in San Antonio with her photographer husband, Michael Nye, and their son, Madison Cloudfeather. Naomi Shihab Nye's stories and poems have been widely anthologized. Her collections of poems include *Different Ways to Pray*, *Hugging the Jukebox*, and *Words Under the Words: Selected Poems.* She has compiled an acclaimed poetry anthology for young readers, *This Same Sky*, and written a picture book, *Sitti's Secrets*, about her Palestinian grandmother. She is also a songwriter and singer.

*Shihab* means shooting star in Arabic.

Shortly after my mother discovered my brother had been pitching his vitamin C tablets behind the stove for years, we left the country. Her sharp alert, "Now the truth be known!" startled us at the breakfast table as she poked into the dim crevice with the nozzle of her vacuum. We could hear the pills go click, click, up the long tube.

My brother, an obedient child, a bright-eyed, dark-skinned charmer who scored high on all his tests and trilled a boy's sweet soprano, stared down at his oatmeal. Four years younger than I, he was also the youngest and smallest in his class. Somehow he maintained an intelligence and dignity more notable than those of his older, larger companions, and the pills episode was really a pleasant surprise to me.

Companions in mischief are not to be underestimated, especially when everything else in your life is about to change.

We sold everything we had and left the country. The move had been brewing for months. We took a few suitcases each. My mother cried when the piano went. I wished we could have saved it. My brother and I had sung so many classics over its keyboard—"Look for the Silver Lining" and "Angels We Have Heard on High," that it would have been nice to return to a year later, when we came straggling back. I sold my life-size doll and my toy sewing machine. I begged my mother to save her red stove for me, so I could have it when I grew up—no one else we knew had a red stove. So my mother asked some friends to save it for me in their barn.

Our parents had closed their imported-gifts stores. Our mother ran a little shop in our neighborhood in St. Louis and our father ran a bigger one in a Sheraton Hotel downtown. For years my brother and I had been sitting with them behind the counters after school, guessing if people who walked through the door would buy something or only browse. We curled with our library books on Moroccan hassocks and Egyptian camel saddles. I loved the stacks of waiting white paper bags as they lay together, and the reams of new tissue. I'd crease the folds as our smooth father in dark suit and daily drench of cologne counted change. Our mother rearranged shelves and penned the perfect tags with calligrapher's ink. My brother and I helped unpack the crates: nested Russian dolls, glossy mother-of-pearl earrings from Bethlehem, a family of sandalwood fans nestled in shredded packaging. Something wonderful was always on its way.

But there were problems too. Sometimes whole days passed and nobody came in. It seemed so strange to wait for people to give you money for what you had. But that's what stores did everywhere. Then the stockroom filled with pre-Christmas inventory caught on fire and burned up, right when our father was between insurance policies. We could hear our parents in the living room, worrying and debating after we went to bed at night. Finally they had to give the business up. What seemed like such a good idea in the beginning—presents from around the world—turned into the sad sound of a broom sweeping out an empty space.

Our father had also been attending the Unity School for Christianity for a few years, but decided not to become a minister after all. We were relieved, having felt like imposters the whole time he was enrolled. He wasn't even a Christian, to begin with, but a gently nonpracticing Muslim. He didn't do anything like fasting or getting down on his knees five times a day. Our mother had given up the stern glare of her Lutheran ancestors, raising my brother and me in the Vedanta Society of St. Louis. When anyone asked what we were, I said, "Hindu." We had a swami, and sandalwood incense. It was over our heads, but we liked it and didn't feel very attracted to the idea of churches and collection baskets and chatty parish good-will.

Now and then, just to keep things balanced, we attended the Unity Sunday School. My teacher said I was lucky my father came from the same place Jesus came from. It was a passport to notoriety. She invited me to bring artifacts for Show and Tell. I wrapped a red and white *keffiyah* around my friend Jimmy's curly blond head while the girls in lacy socks giggled behind their hands. I told about my father coming to America from Palestine on the boat and throwing his old country clothes overboard before docking at Ellis Island. I felt relieved he'd kept a few things, like the *keffiyah* and its black braided band. Secretly it made me mad to have lost the blue pants from Jericho with the wide cuffs he told us about.

I liked standing in front of the group talking about my father's homeland. Stories felt like elastic bands that could stretch and stretch. Big fans purred inside their metal shells. I held up a string of olivewood camels. I didn't tell our teacher about the Vedanta Society. We were growing up ecumenical, though I wouldn't know that word till a long time later in college. One night I heard my father say to my mother in the next room, "Do you think they'll be confused when they grow up?" and knew he was talking about us. My mother, bless her, knew we wouldn't be. She said, "At least we're giving them a choice." I didn't know then that more clearly than all the stories of Jesus,

I'd remember the way our Hindu swami said a single word three times, "*Shanti, shanti, shanti*"—peace, peace, peace.

Our father was an excellent speaker—he stood behind pulpits and podiums easily, delivering gracious lectures on "The Holy Land" and "The Palestinian Question." He was much in demand during the Christmas season. I think that's how he had fallen into the ministerial swoon. While he spoke, my brother and I moved toward the backs of gathering halls, hovering over and eyeing the tables of canapes and tiny tarts, slipping a few into our mouths or pockets.

What next? Our lives were entering a new chapter, but I didn't know its title yet.

We had never met our Palestinian grandmother, Sitti Khadra, or seen Jerusalem, where our father had grown up, or followed the rocky, narrow alleyways of the Via Dolorosa, or eaten an olive in its own neighborhood. Our mother hadn't either. The Arabic customs we knew had been filtered through the fine net of folktales. We did not speak Arabic, though the lilt of the language was familiar to us—our father's endearments, his musical blessings before meals. But that language had never lived in our mouths.

And that's where we were going, to Jerusalem. We shipped our car, a wide golden Impala, over on a boat. We would meet up with it later.

The first plane flight of my whole life was the night flight out of New York City across the ocean. I was fourteen years old. Every glittering light in every skyscraper looked like a period at the end of the sentence. Goodbye, our lives.

We stopped in Portugal for a few weeks. We were making a gradual transition. We stopped in Spain and Italy and Egypt, where the pyramids shocked me by sitting right on the edge of the giant city of Cairo, not way out in the desert as I had imagined them. While we waited for our baggage to clear customs, I stared at six tall African men in brilliantly patterned dashikis negotiating with an Egyptian customs agent and realized I did not even know how to say "thank you" in Arabic. How was this possible? The most elemental and important of human phrases in my father's own tongue had evaded me till now. I tugged on his sleeve, but he was busy with visas and passports. "Daddy," I said. "Daddy, I have to know. Daddy, tell me. Daddy, why didn't we ever *learn?*" An African man adjusted his turban. Always thereafter, the word *shookrun,* so simple, with a little roll in the middle, would conjure up the vast African baggage, the brown boxes looped and looped in African twine.

We stayed one or two nights at the old Shepheard's Hotel downtown but couldn't sleep due to the heat and honking traffic beneath our windows. So our father moved us to the famous Mena House Hotel next to the pyramids. We rode camels for the first time, and our mother received a dozen blood-red roses at her hotel room from a rug vendor who apparently liked her pale brown ponytail. The belly dancer at the hotel restaurant twined a gauzy pink scarf around my brother's astonished ten-year-old head as he tapped his knee in time to her music. She bobbled her giant cleavage under his nose, her huge bosoms prickled by sequins and sweat.

Back in our rooms, we laughed until we fell asleep. Later that night, my brother and I both awakened burning with fever and deeply nauseated, though nobody ever threw up. We were so sick that a doctor hung a Quarantine sign in Arabic and English on our hotel room door the next day. Did he know something we didn't know? I kept waiting to hear that we had malaria or typhoid, but no dramatic disease was ever mentioned. We lay in bed for a week. The aged doctor tripped over my suitcase every time he entered to take our temperatures. We smothered our laughter. "*Shookrun,*" I would say. But as soon as he left, to my brother, "I feel bad. How do you feel?"

"I feel really, really bad."

"I think I'm dying."

"I think I'm already dead."

At night we heard the sound and lights show from the pyramids drifting across the desert air to our windows. We felt our lives stretching out across a thousand miles. The pharaohs stomped noisily through my head and churning belly. We had eaten spaghetti in the restaurant. I would not be able to eat spaghetti again for years.

Finally, finally, we appeared in the restaurant, thin and

weakly smiling, and ordered the famous Mena House *shorraba*, lentil soup, as my brother nervously scanned the room for the belly dancer. Maybe she wouldn't recognize him now.

In those days Jerusalem, which was then a divided city, had an operating airport on the Jordanian side. My brother and I remember flying in upside down, or in a plane dramatically tipped, but it may have been the effect of our medicine. The land reminded us of a dropped canvas, graceful brown hillocks and green patches. Small and provincial, the airport had just two runways, and the first thing I observed as we climbed down slowly from the stuffy plane was all my underwear strewn across one of them. There were my flowered cotton briefs and my pink panties and my slightly embarassing raggedy ones and my extra training bra, alive and visible in the breeze. Somehow my suitcase had popped open in the hold and dropped its contents the minute the men pried open the cargo door. So the first thing I did on the home soil of my father was re-collect my underwear, down on my knees, the posture of prayer over that ancient holy land.

Our relatives came to see us at a hotel. Our grandmother was very short. She wore a long, thickly embroidered Palestinian dress, had a musical, high-pitched voice and a low, guttural laugh. She kept touching our heads and faces as if she couldn't believe we were there. I had not yet fallen in love with her. Sometimes you don't fall in love with people immediately, even if they're your own grandmother. Everyone seemed to think we were all too thin.

We moved into a second-story flat in a stone house eight miles north of the city, among fields and white stones and wandering sheep. My brother was enrolled in the Friends Girls School and I was enrolled in the Friends Boys School in the town of Ramallah a few miles farther north—it all was a little confused. But the Girls School offered grades one through eight in English and high school continued at the Boys School. Most local girls went to Arabic-speaking schools after eighth grade.

I was a freshman, one of seven girl students among two

hundred boys, which would cause me problems a month later. I was called in from the schoolyard at lunchtime, to the office of our counselor who wore shoes so pointed and tight her feet bulged out pinkly on top.

"You will not be talking to them anymore," she said. She rapped on the desk with a pencil for emphasis.

"To whom?"

"All the boy students at this institution. It is inappropriate behavior. From now on, you will speak only with the girls."

"But there are only six other girls! And I like only one of them!" My friend was Anna, from Italy, whose father ran a small factory that made matches. I'd visited it once with her. It felt risky to walk the aisles among a million filled matchboxes. Later we visited the factory that made olive oil soaps and stacked them in giant pyramids to dry.

"No, thank you," I said. "It's ridiculous to say that girls should only talk to girls. Did I say anything bad to a boy? Did anyone say anything bad to me? They're my friends. They're like my brothers. I won't do it, that's all."

The counselor conferred with the headmaster and they called a taxi. I was sent home with a little paper requesting that I transfer to a different school. The charge: insolence. My mother, startled to see me home early and on my own, stared out the window when I told her.

My brother came home from his school as usual, full of whistling and notebooks. "Did anyone tell you not to talk to girls?" I asked him. He looked at me as if I'd gone goofy. He was too young to know the troubles of the world. He couldn't even imagine them.

"You know what I've been thinking about?" he said. "A piece of cake. That puffy white layered cake with icing like they have at birthday parties in the United States. Wouldn't that taste good right now?" Our mother said she was thinking about mayonnaise. You couldn't get it in Jerusalem. She'd tried to make it and it didn't work. I felt too gloomy to talk about food.

My brother said, "Let's go let Abu Miriam's chickens out." That's what we always did when we felt sad. We let our fussy landlord's red-and-white chickens loose to flap around the yard happily, puffing their wings. Even when Abu Miriam shouted and waggled his cane and his wife waved a dishtowel, we knew the chickens were thanking us.

My father went with me to the St. Tarkmanchatz Armenian School, a solemnly ancient stone school tucked deep into the Armenian Quarter of the Old City of Jerusalem. It was another world in there. He had already called the school officials on the telephone and tried to enroll me, though they didn't want to. Their school was for Armenian students only, kindergarten through twelfth grade. Classes were taught in three languages: Armenian, Arabic and English, which was why I needed to go there. Although most Arab students at other schools were learning English, I needed a school where classes were actually taught in English—otherwise I would have been staring out the windows triple the usual amount.

The head priest wore a long robe and a tall cone-shaped hat. He said, "Excuse me, please, but your daughter, she is not an Armenian, even a small amount?"

"Not at all," said my father. "But in case you didn't know, there is a stipulation in the educational code books of this city that says no student may be rejected solely on the basis of ethnic background, and if you don't accept her, we will alert the proper authorities."

They took me. But the principal wasn't happy about it. The students, however, seemed glad to have a new face to look at. Everyone's name ended in *-ian*, the beautiful, musical Armenian ending—Boghossian, Minassian, Kevorkian, Rostomian. My new classmates started calling me Shihabian. We wore uniforms, navy blue pleated skirts for the girls, white shirts, and navy sweaters. I waited during the lessons for the English to come around, as if it were a channel on television. While other students were on the other channels, I scribbled poems in the margins of my pages, read library books, and wrote a lot of letters filled with exclamation points. All the other students knew all three languages with three entirely different alphabets. How could they carry so much in their heads? I felt humbled by my ignorance. One day I felt so frustrated in our physics class—still another language—that I pitched my book out the open window. The professor made me go collect it. All the pages had let loose at the seams and were flapping free into the gutters along with the white wrappers of sandwiches.

Every week the girls had a hands-and-fingernails check. We had to keep our nails clean and trim, and couldn't wear any rings. Some of my new friends would invite me home for lunch with them, since we had an hour-and-a-half break and I lived too far to go to my own house.

Their houses were a thousand years old, clustered beehive-fashion behind ancient walls, stacked and curled and tilting and dark, filled with pictures of unsmiling relatives and small white cloths dangling crocheted edges. We ate spinach pies and white cheese. We dipped our bread in olive oil, as the Arabs did. We ate small sesame cakes, our mouths full of crumbles. They taught me to say "I love you" in Armenian, which sounded like *yes-kay-see-goo-see-rem.* I felt I had left my old life entirely.

Every afternoon I went down to the basement of the school where the kindergarten class was having an Arabic lesson. Their desks were pint-sized, their full white smocks tied around their necks. I stuffed my fourteen-year-old self in beside them. They had rosy cheeks and shy smiles. They must have thought I was a very slow learner.

More than any of the lessons, I remember the way the teacher rapped the backs of their hands with his ruler when they made a mistake. Their little faces puffed up with quiet tears. This pained me so terribly I forgot all my words. When it was my turn to go to the blackboard and write in Arabic, my hand shook. The kindergarten students whispered hints to me from the front row, but I couldn't understand them. We learned horribly useless phrases: "Please hand me the bellows for my fire." I wanted words simple as tools, simple as *food* and *yesterday* and *dreams.* The teacher never rapped my hand, especially after I wrote a letter to the city newspaper, which my father edited, protesting such harsh treatment of young learners. I wish I had known how to talk to those little ones, but they were just beginning their English studies and didn't speak much yet. They were at the same place in their English that I was in my Arabic.

From the high windows of St. Tarkmanchatz, we could look out over the Old City, the roofs and flapping laundry and television antennas, the pilgrims and churches and mosques, the olivewood prayer beads and fragrant *falafel* lunch stands, the intricate interweaving of cultures and prayers and songs and holidays. We saw the barbed wire separating Jordan from Israel then, the bleak, uninhabited strip of no-man's land reminding me how little education saved us after all. People who had differing ideas still came to blows, imagining fighting could solve things. Staring out over the quiet roofs of afternoon, I thought it so foolish. I asked my friends what they thought about it and they shrugged.

"It doesn't matter what we think about it. It just keeps happening. It happened in Armenia too, you know. Really, really bad in Armenia. And who talks about it in the world news now? It happens everywhere. It happens in *your* country one by one, yes? Murders and guns. What can we do?"

Sometimes after school, my brother and I walked up the road that led past the crowded refugee camp of Palestinians who owned even less than our modest relatives did in the village. The little kids were stacking stones in empty tin cans and shaking them. We waved our hands and they covered their mouths and laughed. We wore our beat-up American tennis shoes and our old sweatshirts and talked about everything we wanted to do and everywhere else we wished we could go.

"I want to go back to Egypt," my brother said. "I sort of feel like I missed it. Spending all that time in bed instead of exploring—what a waste."

"I want to go to Greece," I said. "I want to play a violin in a symphony orchestra in Austria." We made up things. I wanted to go back to the United States most of all. Suddenly I felt like a patriotic citizen. One of my friends, Sylvie Markarian, had just been shipped off to Damascus, Syria to marry a man who was fifty years old, a widower. Sylvie was exactly my age—we had turned fifteen two days apart. She had never met her future husband before. I thought this was the most revolting thing I had ever heard of. "Tell your parents no thank you," I urged her. "Tell them you *refuse.*"

Sylvie's eyes were liquid, swirling brown. I could not see clearly to the bottom of them.

"You don't understand," she told me. "In United States you say no. We don't say no. We have to follow someone's wishes. This is the wish of my father. Me, I am scared. I never slept away from my mother before. But I have no choice. I am going because they tell me to go." She was sobbing, sobbing on my shoulder. And I was stroking her long, soft hair. After that, I carried two fists inside, one for Sylvie and one for me.

Most weekends my family went to the village to sit with the relatives. We sat and sat and sat. We sat in big rooms and little rooms, in circles, on chairs or on woven mats or brightly covered mattresses piled on the floor. People came in and out to greet my family. Sometimes even donkeys and chickens came in and out. We were like movie stars or dignitaries. They never seemed to get tired of us.

My father translated the more interesting tidbits of conversation, the funny stories my grandmother told. She talked about angels and food and money and people and politics and gossip and old memories from my father's childhood, before he emigrated away from her. She wanted to make sure we were going to stick around forever, which made me feel very nervous. We ate from mountains of rice and eggplant on large silver trays—they gave us little plates of our own since it was not our custom to eat from the same plate as other people. We ripped the giant wheels of bread into triangles. Shepherds passed through town with their flocks of sheep and goats, their long canes and cloaks, straight out of the Bible. My brother and I trailed them to the edge of the village, past the lentil fields to the green meadows studded with stones, while the shepherds pretended we weren't there. I think they liked to be alone, unnoticed. The sheep had differently colored dyed bottoms, so shepherds could tell their flocks apart.

During these long, slow, smoke-stained weekends—the

men still smoked cigarettes a lot in those days, and the old *taboon*, my family's mounded bread-oven, puffed billowy clouds outside the door—my crying jags began. I cried without any warning, even in the middle of a meal. My crying was usually noiseless but dramatically wet—streams of tears pouring down my cheeks, onto my collar or the back of my hand.

Everything grew quiet.

Someone always asked in Arabic, "What is wrong? Are you sick? Do you wish to lie down?"

My father made valiant excuses in the beginning. "She's overtired," he said. "She has a headache. She is missing her friend who moved to Syria. She is homesick just now."

My brother stared at me as if I had just landed from Planet X.

Worst of all was our drive to school every morning, when our car came over the rise in the highway and all Jerusalem lay sprawled before us in its golden, stony splendor pockmarked with olive trees and automobiles. Even the air above the city had a thick, religious texture, as if it were a shining brocade filled with broody incense. I cried hardest then. All those hours tied up in school lay just ahead. My father pulled over and talked to me. He sighed. He kept his hands on the steering wheel even when the car was stopped and said, "Someday, I promise you, you will look back on this period in your life and have no idea what made you so unhappy here."

"I want to go home." It became my anthem. "This place depresses me. It weighs too much. I hate all these old stones that everybody keeps kissing. I'm sick of pilgrims. They act so pious and pure. And I hate the way people stare at me here." Already I'd been involved in two street skirmishes with boys who stared a little too hard and long. I'd socked one in the jaw and he socked me back. I hit the other one straight in the face with my purse.

"You could be happy here if you tried just a little harder," my father said. "Don't compare it to the United States all the time. Don't pretend the United States is perfect. And look at your brother—he's not having any problems!"

"My brother is eleven years old."

I had crossed the boundary from uncomplicated childhood when happiness was a good ball and a horde of candy-coated Jordan almonds.

One problem was that I had fallen in love with four different boys who all played in the same band. Two of them were even twins. I never quite described it to my parents, but I wrote reams and reams of notes about it on loose-leaf paper that I kept under my sweaters in my closet.

Such new energy made me feel reckless. I gave things away. I gave away my necklace and a whole box of shortbread cookies that my mother had been saving. I gave my extra shoes away to the gypsies. One night when the gypsies camped in a field down the road from our house, I thought about their mounds of white goat cheese lined up on skins in front of their tents, and the wild *oud* music they played deep into the black belly of the night, and I wanted to go sit around their fire. Maybe they could use some shoes.

I packed a sack of old loafers that I rarely wore and walked with my family down the road. The gypsy mothers stared into my shoes curiously. They took them into their tent. Maybe they would use them as vases or drawers. We sat with small glasses of hot, sweet tea until a girl bellowed from deep in her throat, threw back her head, and began dancing. A long bow thrummed across the strings. The girl circled the fire, tapping and clicking, trilling a long musical wail from deep in her throat. My brother looked nervous. He was remembering the belly dancer in Egypt, and her scarf. I felt invisible. I was pretending to be a gypsy. My father stared at me. Didn't I recognize the exquisite oddity of my own life when I sat right in the middle of it? Didn't I feel lucky to be here? Well, yes I did. But sometimes it was hard to be lucky.

When we left Jerusalem, we left quickly. Left our beds in our rooms and our car in the driveway. Left in a plane, not sure where we were going. The rumbles of fighting with Israel had been growing louder and louder. In the barbed-wire no-man's land visible from the windows of our house, guns cracked loudly in the middle of the night. We lived right near the edge. My father heard disturbing rumors at the newspaper that would soon grow into the infamous Six Day War of 1967. We were in England by then, drinking tea from thin china cups and scanning the newspapers. Bombs were blowing up in Jerusalem. We worried about the village. We worried about my grandmother's dreams, which had been getting worse and worse, she'd told us. We worried about the house we'd left, and the chickens, and the children at the refugee camp. But there was nothing we could do except keep talking about it all.

My parents didn't want to go back to Missouri because they'd already said goodbye to everyone there. They thought we might try a different part of the country. They weighed the virtues of different states. Texas was big and warm. After a chilly year crowded around the small gas heaters we used in Jerusalem, a warm place sounded appealing. In roomy Texas, my parents bought the first house they looked at. My father walked into the city newspaper and said, "Any jobs open around here?"

I burst out crying when I entered a grocery store—so many different kinds of bread.

A letter on thin blue airmail paper reached me months later, written by my classmate, the bass player in my favorite Jerusalem band. "Since you left," he said, "your empty desk reminds me of a snake ready to strike. I am afraid to look at it. I hope you are having a better time than we are."

Of course I was, and I wasn't. *Home* had grown different forever. *Home* had doubled. Back *home* again in my own country, it seemed impossible to forget the place we had just left: the piercing call of the *muezzin* from the mosque at prayer time, the dusky green tint of the olive groves, the sharp, cold air that smelled as deep and old as my grandmother's white sheets flapping from the line on her roof. What story hadn't she finished?

Our father used to tell us that when he was little, the sky over Jerusalem crackled with meteors and shooting stars almost every night. They streaked and flashed, igniting the dark. Some had long golden tails. For a few seconds, you could see their whole swooping trail lit up. Our father and his brothers slept on the roof to watch the sky. "There were so many of them, we didn't even call out every time we saw one."

During our year in Jerusalem, my brother and I kept our eyes cast upwards whenever we were outside at night, but the stars were different since our father was a boy. Now the sky seemed too orderly, stuck in place. The stars had learned where they belonged. Only people on the ground kept changing.

# ACKNOWLEDGMENTS


The publisher gratefully acknowledges and thanks the authors, publishers, and literary agents for their contributions to this volume.

JUDITH ORTIZ COFER: "One More Lesson," from *Silent Dancing: A Partial Remembrance of a Puerto Rican Childhood* by Judith Ortiz Cofer, copyright © 1989 by Judith Ortiz Cofer (Houston: Arte Publico Press–University of Houston, 1989). Reprinted by permission of the publisher.

LEE A. DANIELS: "A Boston Latin School Boy," copyright © 1995 by Lee A. Daniels. First published in *Going Where I'm Coming From*, by arrangemen vith the author.

HELEN EPSTEIN: "Dinnertime" (Chapter Four), from *Children of the Holocaust* (Putnam, 1979; Penguin, 1980) by Helen Epstein, copyright © 1979 by Helen Epstein. Reprinted by permission of the author.

TRACY MARX: "Absolutely Someday," copyright © 1995 by Tracy Marx. First published in *Going Where I'm Coming From*, by arrangement with the author.

VED MEHTA: Excerpt from *Sound-Shadows of the New World* by Ved Mehta, copyright © 1985 by Ved Mehta. Reprinted by permission of W. W. Norton & Company, Inc.

THYLIAS MOSS: "Wings," copyright © 1995 by Thylias Moss. First published in *Going Where I'm Coming From*, by arrangement with the author.

LENSEY NAMIOKA: "Math and Aftermath" is excerpted from a work in progress, *Life with Chaos: Growing Up with a Chinese Father*, by Lensey Namioka, copyright © 1995 by Lensey Namioka; for rights information, contact Ruth Cohen, Inc., Literary Agent. First published in *Going Where I'm Coming From*, by arrangement with the author.

NAOMI SHIHAB NYE: "Thank You in Arabic," copyright © 1995 by Naomi Shihab Nye. First published in *Going Where I'm Coming From*, by arrangement with the author.

SUSAN POWER: "Stone Women," copyright © 1991 by Susan Power. First published in *Iowa Woman*. Reprinted by permission of Harold Ober Associates, Inc.

LUIS J. RODRÍGUEZ: Excerpt from *Always Running, La Vida Loca: Gang Days in L.A.*, copyright © 1993 by Luis J. Rodríguez, reprinted by permission of Curbstone Press, 321 Jackson Street, Willimantic, CT 06226.

WILLIE RUFF: Excerpt from *A Call to Assembly: The Autobiography of a Musical Storyteller*, copyright © 1991 by Willie Ruff, reprinted by permission of Viking Penguin, a division of Penguin USA.

GRAHAM SALISBURY: "Ice," copyright © 1995 by Graham Salisbury. First published in *Going Where I'm Coming From*, by arrangement with the author.

GARY SOTO: "One More Time," copyright © 1985 by Gary Soto, from *Living Up the Street*. Reprinted by permission of the author.

HISAYE YAMAMOTO: "The Enormous Piano," copyright © 1977 by Hisaye Yamamoto Desoto. First published in somewhat different form in *Rafu Shimpo*. Reprinted by arrangement with the author.